Listen Up—God Talking!

Listen Up—God Talking!

◆

An introduction to biblical living

James F. Miller

iUniverse, Inc.
New York Lincoln Shanghai

Listen Up—God Talking!
An introduction to biblical living

iUniverse books may be ordered through booksellers or by contacting:

iUniverse
2021 Pine Lake Road, Suite 100
Lincoln, NE 68512
www.iuniverse.com
1-800-Authors (1-800-288-4677)

ISBN: 0-595-33813-5 (pbk)
ISBN: 0-595-67015-6 (cloth)

Printed in the United States of America

To my children and their loved ones:
that they may know
what I have been doing
with my life.

Contents

PREFACE

Of the writing of books there is no end. This is especially true of books on the Bible. In itself this fact is instructive, for the Bible holds so much meaning, nuance, and adventure that there will never be enough books written to make all it contains clear and obvious. Such is my meager excuse for offering this, yet another, introductory book on reading the Bible.

I have other reasons.

I am of the view that many, perhaps most, of all the introductory books written for the interested lay person fail to reveal the astonishing challenges of the Bible. There is something predictable, even pallid about them. I hope to penetrate this pallid predictability in the pages that follow. The Bible is neither predictable nor pallid, and its edge must be heard and seen. Hiding the edge from lay readers is in fact an act of dishonesty by those who know better, the many authors of such books.

Another reason: over three decades in active ministry have shown me a disturbing fact of life amongst adult church membership. They are (with many fine exceptions) biblically illiterate. Many have a nodding acquaintance with this or that story, event, or character, but most are lost in grasping the biblical message *as a whole*. The wholeness of Scripture eludes them. Christian Education curricula are mainly to blame for this.[1] Most curricula do not follow the Bible story from start to finish, instead dividing the material in such a way (usually in teaching quarters) that Paul may follow David, Moses come after Jesus, and the early church flow out of Adam and Eve. It is a method designed to destroy comprehension.

For those faithful folks who do come to adult Bible studies far too often their first response when asked about the meaning of what is being read is to quote the "study guide" material rather than read the text. They do not trust the biblical words to speak to them without "life application" helps from the collective wisdom of what I call "Professor Gumpelheimer."[2] Study Bibles are tremendous helps, but not if they control, limit, and condition the spontaneous response to the scriptural text. (My wife refers to such Bibles as "bossy Bibles.") My aim in the Bible studies I lead and in this book is for you to set Gumpelheimer aside and allow the text to speak. You will need to read this book with a Bible by your side.[3]

In the appendix I offer an outline, based on visual aids, for the contents of an Old Testament curriculum which would be designed to reveal its structure as a whole and thereby provide the context for the New Testament. (I will subsequently be offering a similar outline for a New Testament curriculum.) This book itself, however, is designed to bring a cohesive vision of the entire Bible into focus. The appendix is merely intended as supplemental. If visual aids do not appeal to you simply ignore the appendix.

Ever since my college and seminary years I have wrestled with the Bible and sought to bring its meaning to ordinary people. I have always said that if you take away my Bible I have nothing to say or at least nothing anyone should listen to. This book is the result of my experience—in reading, reflecting upon, and applying. William Barclay, the late popularizer of the New Testament who was professor of New Testament when I studied at Glasgow University, used to insist that all life's questions could be illuminated, if not directly answered, by viewing them biblically. "Biblicality" was the philosophy he insisted upon. "Willie B." instilled in all who studied under him a deep appreciation of the power of the Bible's words as they are found in their original languages. A New Testament class with Barclay demanded not only the obvious facility with Greek but an ability to look into Hebrew as well, not to mention Latin. This biblicality with its language-based approach will be obvious in the coming pages.

Another Glasgow professor, Ronald Gregor Smith, also made a huge impact on me. The original translator of Buber's I and Thou, "Gregor" as we students referred to him, not daring the "Ronnie" of his intimates, was quiet but insistent. His manner was slow infiltration. His tone of voice was impossible to shut out. I can hear him now: "Theology must learn to be more modest." Modest? Say and pretend less.

In addition to Barclay and Smith there have been countless other influences that have impacted my thinking, not least of which are the works of Martin Buber, Geza Vermes, Karl Barth, and Dietrich Bonhoeffer.

Apart from authors and scholars, however, I want to acknowledge the many participants in classes I have taught over the years, both in church and college settings. A student's questioning is a mighty stimulus to clarity and a ruthless destroyer of smug imprecision. I am indebted to many such questioning encounters.

I am especially indebted, above all else, to my wife Karen. Not only is she a fine editor with a keen appreciation of written English (and the precise demands that go with that appreciation) she is also the most biblically literate and spiritually perceptive person I know. She spots humbug a mile away and is encyclopedic in her scriptural knowledge, in the broadest sense, placing the Bible in the wider context of Christian reflection over the centuries. Additionally, with her astonishing breadth of reading in literature and cultural development, she is even better able to advise and correct. My debt to her cannot be paid, but perhaps this book goes some way towards thanking her for all she is, as advisor and editor, wife and companion. She has made my life possible.

1

How to listen to the Bible

What is the Bible?

This seems to be an odd question. If you are reading these words you are doing so because you have some idea of what the Bible is. You might think the Bible is

- a book that contains the holy Word of God.

- a book used by the church to lead, inspire, and/or control.

- a book that shows us how to live a right and good life.

- a book about Jesus.

Notice what all of these have in common. They all refer to the Bible as "a book."

This is hardly surprising. The Greek word *biblos* means "book"; the Bible looks like a book; you can buy one in the bookstore; and you can read it just like a book. But take a look at its table of contents. What do we find in most tables of contents? Usually there is a list of chapters with individual titles, and often a structure or plot is revealed. Not so with the Bible's table of contents. There isn't a list of chapters at all. What kind of list do we find? A list of books.

The Bible is not *a* book. The Bible is a collection of books.

Think about that for a moment. The Bible is a collection of books. Certain questions immediately come to mind:

- Who collected the books?

- When, where, and why were they collected?

- What purpose did the individual books serve before they were put into the collection? Were they being read regularly, or had they been lost for a while?

- When, where, and why were the individual books written?

Another look at the Bible's table of contents reveals that the books are presented in two major sub-collections called by Christians the "Old Testament" and the "New Testament." The Old Testament derives its name in reference to the New Testament, but the books in the Old Testament were not written and collected by people who knew that another "testament" would follow. Why then were these older books gathered? What were they, and what was their significance before they became "old" in relation to the "new"? Was the meaning of these individual books and then their collection as a whole somehow changed when they were placed in the relation of "old" to "new"?[4] Besides, what is a "testament"?

How can we ever expect the Bible to give us purpose and guidance for our lives when even this cursory glance at its table of contents raises so many questions? Is the task hopeless?

The task, of course, is not hopeless. But, in order to find our way into the Bible's message, to avoid imposing our own message onto it or squeezing our preconceived notions into it, we need to keep in mind certain key biblical realities. Forget these realities and we mislead ourselves.

The Five Realities of the Bible

- First, there is the Bible's age.

Scholars debate and disagree over many of the finer points of dating this or that biblical passage or book, but a broad consensus does emerge. The Bible recounts events ranging from 2,000 BCE to 100 CE.[5] Think about it. The closest events to us occurred over 1900 years ago. Over a millennium—nearly two millennia. The most remote events were taking place over three times that length from the present time. How utterly extraordinary it is that we still read such an ancient book in order to gain insight into the complexities and challenges of our modern life. Yet, that is precisely what countless people do and what every church claims we ought to do. When we consider how to go about reading the Bible we have to find a process that takes into account the Bible's age and enables it to speak to the contemporary world. It wouldn't be at all surprising if parts of such an ancient book seemed irrelevant to us. Indeed, it would be astonishing if it were otherwise.

• Second, there are the Bible's languages.

With the exception of a small portion of Daniel, which was written in Aramaic, the Bible was written in two languages, the Old Testament in Hebrew and the New Testament in Greek. The Hebrew is similar to, but not identical with, the Hebrew spoken in Israel today. A modern Israeli could easily read the Hebrew part of the Bible, but an ancient Hebrew reader would not be able to converse on the streets of Tel Aviv without a lot of extra training. Biblical Greek is sometimes called "common" Greek. It is a simpler, less structured, and less literary version of the Greek of ancient classical Greece. Again, a Greek resident of ancient Athens could have read the New Testament in the original, but today's seminarian trained to read the New Testament would struggle with the Athens daily newspaper. In deciding how to understand the Bible we have to consider the reality of its ancient languages.

What this means for those of us who read the Bible in English is that, between us and the page, between us and the words, between us and "the Word," there are *invisible partners*. These invisible partners have made decisions, adopted a philosophy, and have even introduced a theological point of view. I am speaking, of course, about the translators, those highly skilled people who work with the source languages and shoot for clear expression in English, our target language. Not all translators have the same method or approach. Knowing the translators' point of view or language philosophy is critical when we are choosing a Bible. Do the translators hold the view, for example, that the same biblical word (Hebrew or Greek) should always be translated by the same English word, or do they phrase their translation the way the source-language idiom seems to require? Moreover, as spoken and written English evolves, so too do the translations of the Bible. The old King James Version does not use today's English. Many readers have moved on to newer, more modern translations.[6]

• Third, there is the Bible's text.

What original documents do translators have to work with? Printing was not invented until the sixteenth century by Gutenberg. This event is sometimes referred to as the most crucial event in our civilization's development. Prior to printing, books were handwritten. That is what "manuscript" means—written (*scripto* in Latin) by hand (*manus* in Latin). There are thousands of manuscripts in Hebrew and Greek for translators to work with. But, remember this: there is not one single original manuscript of the entire Bible in the original languages. More, there is not one single original manuscript of the entire Old or New Testament in its original language. The texts of these testaments, and therefore the text of the whole Bible, have to be pieced together from the best manuscripts available.

In other words, the Bible behind the translation you read is a compilation. To compile or create the best text scholars have to weigh the value of one manuscript against another. If a manuscript seems to have something written in the margin, for example, should they conclude these words were part of the original that had been overlooked and then added in later as a correction? Or, were those words the comment of that particular manuscript's scribe, added in as speculation? Textual problems abound.

- Fourth, there are the Bible's cultures.

The Bible not only tells of people and events from long ago but of people and events from historical, geographical, social, moral, and economic situations far removed from the twenty-first century. Think of a time and place that was pre-industrial, pre-democratic, pre-technological, pre-psychological, in many cases pre-agricultural and pre-urban and you will have in view the world of the Bible. The cultures of the Bible were more in tune with pharaohs and emperors than with presidents and prime ministers; with camels and donkeys than with automobiles and airplanes; with open flames and well water than with microwaves and dishwashers; with messengers from afar than with the cell phones or e-mail. When we consider how to read the Bible we cannot ignore the reality of its underlying cultures. Sometimes they will have to be explained and at other times ignored.[7]

- Fifth, there are the Bible's genres.

The Bible is made up of a series of books. Not all the books are alike, even within each of the two testaments. In the New Testament, for example, there are "gospels" and letters; in the Old Testament there are history books and other books that appear to be poetic discourses. The nature of the Bible's vastly differing constituent parts needs to be taken seriously. For example, we do not read a love poem with the same passion for literal meaning that we use to read the annual report of a company. Depending on the genre our mode of comprehension changes. This is true of the Bible also. We must always adjust the manner of our reading to take account of the genre before us.

Furthermore, not all of the books were written at the same time, in the same place, for the same audience, for the same purpose. The contents were put together over time.

The Bible is a redaction. *A redaction is the end result of a process of collecting and editing.*

What controlled the editing and collecting process? Who did it? When? Why? Were there more than one editing steps? If so, what was the last one? This last one, after all, would have had the opportunity to put a final spin on the whole.

These five fundamental realities have to be kept in mind as we read any biblical passage. They can, in the meantime, be used to prompt three rules for sound Bible reading.

The Three Rules for Sound Bible Reading

- Rule One: The words we read are never the final measure of meaning for the written passage.

When we read the Bible in English we are not reading the words as they were originally written. The literal meaning of the words we read is the literal meaning in English. For example, in John 6: 7 we read in the New International Version that the value of the bread needed to feed the five thousand was "eight month's wages." In the New Revised Version the value is given as "six month's wages." Which is it, six or eight? Obviously, we are not supposed to take these words (six and eight) literally. The original Greek gives a value in the coinage of the day—two hundred denarii—and the translators have tried to take this "source" value and give us a "target" value that makes sense today. The disagreement between "eight" and "six" has nothing to do with "what the Bible says," and everything to do with the translator's view of inflation. As far as the meaning of the passage goes, it matters not a whit whether it says six or eight months. The point is that a huge amount of money was needed, which emphasizes the size of the crowd and the scope of the miracle of Jesus. While this is a trivial example it illustrates something that repeatedly occurs, often with much more profound implications. We can never assume that the words we read are the final measure of meaning for the passage. Taking the whole Bible literally is just plain irresponsible.

- Rule Two: Never make a text answer a question it is not asking.

If we accept that the Bible is a redaction (the end result of a process of collecting and editing many different texts from many different situations) it follows that individual books and, indeed, individual passages might have differing purposes, even from the redaction as a whole. To illustrate, consider the morning newspaper.

Two men meet on the morning commuter train. One has the daily paper. His friend asks about the big game from the previous night. He wants to know the score and how it played out. The man with the newspaper hands him the business section, inviting him to read about it for himself. The business section? How will that help? Will the sports enthusiast get the information he wants? Obviously not. In order to find out about the big game he needs to read the sports section. The business section will tell him about the stock market and the like. If that had been his interest it would have been perfect. As it is, what should he do with his question and the wrong section of the paper? Should he somehow try to interpret the long lists of opening and closing share prices as if they were a secret code about the score of last night's big game? Such a response would clearly be ridiculous. The business section is not written to tell how the big game went. In order to find the answer to his question, the man must read the part of the paper intended to answer it, namely the sports section. It is so obvious.

Never make a text answer a question it is not asking. A love letter is one thing; an essay on the problem of the hermeneutical circle another. Sadly, in the case of the Bible too many people break this fundamental rule and try, using arcane and weird methods, to make a biblical passage answer questions it was never meant to address.[8] If all we want is to hear ourselves think or to have our prior prejudices confirmed we can do what we like with the Bible. If, on the other hand, we want to give ourselves the best chance to hear what the Bible has to say we must never make the Bible, or any biblical passage, answer a question it is not asking.

- Rule Three: A text without a context is a pretext.

Isaiah 2:4 speaks of war and advises people to "beat their swords into plowshares." Joel 3:9–11 also addresses the same issue and advises people to "beat their plowshares into swords." What are we to conclude?—that the Bible contradicts itself? That God cannot make up his mind on the war issue? That the Bible is mindless and should be ignored? Before coming to any of these conclusions we must pause and consider that the Bible has been read with thoughtful interest and keen examination by countless people over many centuries. Obviously there is "something there." So, when a puzzle such as the Isaiah/Joel conflict appears we must remember that the key to it is in the contexts of the two passages. What was the situation addressed by Isaiah? Was it the same as that of Joel? Is there something in these two contexts that, once understood, allows us to hear both texts afresh and speaking some unifying word? A text without a context is a pre-text. Pacifists and warmongers alike often ignore the context issue and use which-ever of these two texts they want to support their prior opinions and points of view. This is to do radical disservice to the Bible.

There are four dimensions to the power and importance of context.

1. *The context in life*: This refers to the historical setting in which the words were first uttered. Sometimes this setting is clear and sometimes it is obscure. If the historical setting is obscure it can sometimes be reconstructed and recovered. In some cases it cannot.

2. *The context in the book*: Why is it, for example, that passage B comes after A and before C. By placing it there does the author (or the redactor) want it to be read in a certain way?

3. *The context of the intended audience*: What did the original hearers or readers of the words expect, and how were they going to react? Did they have certain needs, problems, or expectations that colored the words themselves? Again, some-times this context can be gathered from the evidence and sometimes not.

4. *The context of the reader* (That's you and me): What assumptions and pre-suppositions do we bring to our reading? The hardest of these to detect are those most ingrained. Serious Bible reading requires a radical kind of honesty with our-selves. Are we prepared to be challenged, surprised, and disturbed? Are we willing to have some of our cherished views threatened?

Summary

We must listen carefully to the Bible. Only in this way we will be able to hear the wonderful, amazing, challenging, comforting message it has to give us. How we can effectively listen to the Bible is the challenge this book will address. This, however, is only the first step in a more complex challenge.

Having learned to listen, we must then discover how to pay attention and hav-ing discovered how to pay attention we must identify how to speak. These two other tasks will be dealt with in a companion volume, *Speak Up—Faith Talking! an invitation to biblical living*. For now, learning to listen is a big enough chal-lenge.

The task before us in this book is to hear "what the Bible says." If we faithfully strive after this objective, we will be rewarded by hearing "what God says."

Notice very carefully: *the Bible does not speak with one voice*. Churches claim that the Bible speaks the "Word of God." This may well be so, yet that Word is uttered in a rich variety of ways. This is an important point. The voices in it are human voices, contained in words scripted by human beings. In a very real sense all we have before us on the pages of the Bible are the responses of people to their experiences—experiences they believed were manifestations of some kind. This is in sharp contrast to the Muslim view of the *Koran*, which, Islam claims, is the record of the very Arabic language sounds Muhammad heard from Gabriel, Allah's angelic messenger. (*Koran* derives from the Arabic for "recite." The very title, in other words, is a proclamation that Muhammad merely recited what he heard. Indeed, one of the titles given to him in Islam is "the illiterate" to make this very point.) This is not the case with the biblical authors. They wrote, composed, edited, and collected.

Again, notice very carefully: the Bible seeks to answer very specific questions. There are some who assume that a holy book that claims supernatural authority of some kind ought to have explicit answers to every conceivable question. This is ridiculous. You will never find a chapter and verse in the Bible that deals explicitly with late-term abortion, corporate greed, or thermonuclear war. Verses can be twisted to provide answers to such questions, but this kind of twisting ignores the five realities and three rules outlined above. *It is easy to make the Bible say what we want it to say. It is far more difficult to ensure that we have heard what it wants us to hear.* The Bible is not a physics or a biology manual, nor is it a bio-ethical textbook. It seeks to answer specific questions and address specific needs. We must identify these specific questions and needs to have any chance of hearing the Bible's answering voices. It is only once these voices have been truly heard and understood that the "biblicality" Professor Barclay espoused can then be carried into the debate about other issues and concerns that seem to lack clear biblical directive.

The Bible uses a variety of tones and texts to answer the fundamental questions it raises. This variety ought to reassure us. There are times when one voice may strike us as more authentic, closer to our need. Clinging to that voice does not mean that we are rejecting the others. It merely indicates a focus. A change in our circumstances will prompt us to move to another voice. This can be a repeating pattern, and as our life changes, develops, and grows, the entire scope of scriptural witness can be absorbed.

In other words, we have to engage in a constant process of assessment and evaluation. We must learn not only to interpret the Bible but also to evaluate it. Does what it says here or there actually apply to us any longer? Can this or that passage, if examined with any integrity at all, reflect the will of a God we would want to have faith in?

2

The Question and the Need (Genesis 1–11)

Beginnings

The book of Genesis claims to be "the beginning" (Gen. 1:1). This beginning is, in fact, many beginnings—of Creation, of the Torah, of the Old Testament, of the Bible, of Israel, of Judaism, of Islam, and of Christianity. To embark on reading Genesis is to stand at a "beginning" of a comprehensive and radical kind, one that embraces another, more personal kind of beginning—of adventure, of challenge, and of new perspective on faith and life. To read Genesis is to discover that we are being read. Our assumptions about the meaning of these ancient stories will be confronted, and our ideas of God, the world, and the human adventure may well be turned upside down. Reading Genesis can and should become the beginning of a new you.

Scholars—Jewish, Christian, Muslim, and secular—have studied Genesis for centuries. There are as many views about all the questions this book generates as we can imagine. The purposes of our reading need not be determined by any one of these debates, but from time to time specialists' insights can be useful in helping us avoid blind alleys. We should keep in mind the following general points gleaned from scholarship as we read the Genesis passages.

Sources and Sense

The first five books of the Old Testament—Genesis, Exodus, Leviticus, Numbers, and Deuteronomy—are sometimes referred to as the Pentateuch, derived from the Greek word for "five." The Jews call them "the Torah." Both these names show us that in some sense the five books are viewed as a whole, as some kind of unit.

As scholars examined this unit over the last two centuries or so, they began to discern different strands within it. These strands are spoken of as J, D, E, and P.

Each letter indicates a different strand of tradition and material that has been woven with the others into the whole that is now before us as five separate books. (Some scholars believe these strands of tradition might carry on into Joshua. In this case they then speak of the Hexateuch, after the Greek word for "six.")

When these strands were first identified and isolated scholars assumed they had once existed as separate and independent written sources. Nowadays they are viewed more as trends of thought, trajectories of tradition, and clusters of community memory. A given strand did not, in other words, come into being on a set publication date like the latest best-seller-to-be. Evolving over time, being added to as experience warranted, each strand has its own emphasis, point of view, and even, very probably, its own geographical and demographic origin. A thumbnail sketch of these strands is as follows:

J stems from the Tetragrammaton YHWH. (The German transliteration is JHWH—hence the J—and since most of the pioneer scholars were Germans the usage has stuck.) YHWH was the ancient sacred name for God, revealed to Moses on Horeb during the burning-bush episode in Exodus 3. (Sometimes you will see this word written as Yahweh, but more usually as "LORD"—printed out with small capital letters. There are good reasons for not using Yahweh as we will see when we look closely at Exodus 3.) Following the death of Solomon Israel was split into two separate kingdoms. The northern was called Israel and the southern, Judah. The J strand is sometimes identified with the tribes that comprised the southern kingdom of Judah. Some scholars believe that these tribes, in fact, were the only ones to go through the slavery-Exodus-wilderness-Sinai-covenant experience.

E stands for *elohim*, a plural form of the common Semitic word for "the divine." The word *el* is found in the names of many places (for example, Bethel is the "house of God") and many people (for example, Elimelech is "God is my king.") This Semitic sound also lies behind the Arabic word "Allah." It is not a name so much as a designation or recognition of the divine. In the E strand God as *el* is more distant than in the J strand where God is personal, immediate, and known by his name, YHWH. The E strand is often identified with the Northern Kingdom of Israel.

D stems from the word Deuteronomy. It identifies a strand that stresses the centrality of Jerusalem and the importance of this city's single shrine or temple in the life of the nation. It often echoes certain prophetic themes found elsewhere in the Hebrew Bible. It is represented supremely in Deuteronomy 12–26. This section of the Bible is sometimes thought to be the ancient book found during temple renovations, as recounted in 2 Kings 22.

P stands for the word "priestly." This strand reflects the point of view of the priests of ancient Israel. The priests were responsible for maintaining the cult, and they regarded the nation's ritual integrity as of supreme importance. The central interests of the priestly strand are worship, sacrifice, seasonal observances, matters of purity, and the like. In other words, the strand stems from the religious institutional professionals.

Redaction and Spin

As we noted earlier, a book put together from various sources is called a "redaction."

Imagine you are in charge of a group that has to write a report outlining a company's priorities for the coming business cycle. The report is to be wide-ranging and comprehensive. Your writers are each given areas of the company to assess and review. As editor, however, you have a particular point of view, an area of the company's life with which you are most familiar and which, as a matter of fact, you regard to be the most essential. The various reports reach your desk. You set about the task of compilation. To your dismay you note that your own favorite area is underplayed. By carefully placing the various articles in a certain order, and by using eye-catching fonts, headlines, and pictures, you create a bias. Then you compose your introduction. Your power to create an impression, to put a spin on the entire report, is immense. You are a redactor. Clearly, the redactor can control the lasting impression of the whole.

Who was the redactor of the Pentateuch and—of special interest to us at the moment—of Genesis?

- In Genesis the J and P strands predominate.

- Did the redactor belong to one of these traditions, or did he represent the strand E or D?

- Would it not help us to know who, from which tradition, put the final spin on the entire unit?

The consensus view today amongst Old Testament scholars is that the Pentateuch or Torah redaction was created in response to the challenges of an enormous crisis in Israel's life. In the early sixth century BCE, the Babylonian Exile, about which we will be learning more below, brought Israel to the point of self-doubt and deep uncertainty. If a text without a context is a pretext, the immediate context *for the redaction* was this time of crisis. This scholarly consensus also maintains that the P school of thought was the redacting power.

The importance of this theory is that it draws to our attention a foundational idea, one noted by many theologians. This is the concept of "the midst." Redactors do not redact for the fun of it. They are prompted by some reason; something occurs that seems to cry out for a new take on the past, a new vision of the future. The more we recognize that the Bible—or in the case we are looking at, the Pentateuch—is a redaction, the more important it becomes for us to understand the redactors' situation. Where had they come from? Where were they? What were they trying to tell their readers? What was the broad context of their experience? The "midst" idea addresses these questions.

Consider Jesus. Nowhere do Christians assert that he arrived out of the blue. He came to prominence in the midst of Israel with its ancient, established traditions. Something had already been started there. Later, Paul's great ministry challenge was to take the Christ event into the midst of Greek and Roman culture. Christian theology has been engaged in a similar task ever since—bringing Christ into the midst of wherever Christians happen to find themselves.

"The midst" is the place of God's ongoing dealings with the world and specifically with humanity. (See Figure 4 in the appendix.)

This same reality is found in Israel's story. Israel's great saving event is the cluster of episodes now known collectively as the Exodus. The Exodus, like the ministry and mission of Jesus, did not come out of the blue, but into the midst. There was a community of people already on history's stage, dealing with life under God and trying to discern his will for them and the world.

Genesis is Israel's "midst." From a New Testament perspective, a crass way of putting it is that Genesis is to Israel as the entire story of Israel is to Christ.

If this is so, that Genesis is Israel's midst—it recounts the tale of a people already engaged with God—we must surely look a little more closely at the structure of Genesis.

Structure and Meaning

A quick reading of Genesis cannot fail to reveal a change in tone and atmosphere at the beginning of chapter 12. From that point on, and throughout the remainder of the book, a specificity of time, place, and character is apparent or at least suggested, something that is totally absent from the first 11 chapters. Chapters 12 to 50 are dominated by three towering figures: Abraham, Jacob, and Joseph. They strike us as being specific characters. They jump off the page. They engage us. Isaac seems to play a more minor role than the others, serving only as a link between Abraham and Jacob. (By the way, this may not be and, in my opinion, is not the correct reading of the Isaac figure's role. However, to develop this thought would lead us away from our main objective.) Based on these three figures, therefore, chapters 12 to 50 of Genesis can be structured as follows:

The Abraham Stories:	12–25:18
The Jacob Stories:	25:19–36:43
The Joseph Stories:	37–50

Even these stories, however, come "in the midst." The call to Abram in chapter 12 does not come out of nowhere. Something is already going on. This "something" is contained in the first eleven chapters. If Genesis is the midst for Israel's saving event, then Genesis 1–11 is the midst for Genesis 12–50. And remember what we noted at the outset. Genesis is the beginning of everything. Thus, chapters 1-11 must be the midst for everything that follows.

These eleven chapters are elusive. The kind of specificity of time, place, and person we noted in the Abraham, Jacob, and Joseph stories is missing. Where was the Garden? The Tower? The Flood? Who was Cain, and where did his wife come from? Did serpents really talk to humans in those days? The entire tone of the stories in these first eleven chapters is unlike anything else in Genesis (and unlike anything in the rest of the Bible until Revelation).

Scholars identify two types of material in 1–11: narratives and genealogies. (There is one section, however, marked in italics below, that can fall under either or both.) It is helpful to read the two types as units themselves rather than consecutively as they are found in the Bible. In this way the first chapters of Genesis can be structured as follows:

Genealogies:	*1–2:4a*; 4:1–2, 4:17–26; 5; 6:9–10; 9:28–29; 10; 11:10–32	
Narratives:	*1–2:4a*	Creation
	2:4b–3	Garden
	4:3–16	Brothers
	6:1–9:27	Flood
	11:1–9	Tower

This quick analysis of the shape of Genesis ought to raise some issues in our minds. Why did the P redactor put it together this way? (Remember our editor who had the last say on the final shape of the company's report?) Does "the midst" of chapters 1–11 present something *as a whole* to which the rest of Israel's history is in some sense a response? If so, maybe what we have thought or been taught to think about these chapters misses the point. Might it be the case that we have never really heard what they are actually saying?

Questions and Archetypal Stories

A book is written, a story is told, and a tradition is passed on *for a reason*. As readers of a book, hearers of a story, or participants in a tradition we must determine what that reason is. The reason will be the book's or the story's or the tradition's "message."

Only when the message has been discerned are we in a position to pass a value judgment. This value judgment, in turn, will be based on how well the message can be applied to our lives now. Then again, perhaps we may find we can hear the message and see its implications for our lives, but do not like it. That may color our value judgment as well. Sometimes our reason for reading is not at all the reason behind the writing. This is fine, so long as this fact is recognized—that we are reading with an aim in view other than finding out what the author intended.

A classic example of such a book being read for reasons very different from the author's intention is *Robinson Crusoe*. Published in the seventeenth century in the midst of literal life-and-death struggles between Protestants and Roman Catholics, Defoe's intention was to offer a defense of the fundamental Protestant point of view. A man, stranded with only a Bible to help him, could find salvation without the intermediary help of a priest. Nowadays, the story is read differently—as the story of a shipwrecked man being rescued rather than as a parable of salvation. There is nothing wrong with reading Crusoe this way so long as we do not assume it was Defoe's original intent. If we want to know what Defoe had in mind, however, we need to probe more deeply.

These observations apply to all art. We may feel bewildered or disgusted by a work of art in a gallery, but we don't take this very seriously. When we read the Bible, however, we do so in the belief that the message we hear is in some way supposed to impact our lives. This certainly makes our reading a lot more challenging and threatening. As we look at the various portions and sections that make up Genesis, therefore, our primary task, though not our final one, is to enquire about its reason for being there in front of us. Why has this been written and handed down? What question was the teller of this tale trying to answer?

Some questions cannot be answered—the ones nobody knows the answers to, for example. But, even questions we do know the answers to sometimes cannot be answered fully. "Mommy, do you love me? What do I mean to you?" What mother, when asked such questions, can believe her answer will ever capture the depths of her feelings for her child? A mother can use words to answer, of course, but in her heart she knows that what she really wants to say cannot be said. Words do not capture the truth of the matter. In a very real sense all words fall short. All our language is a "feeling after" what we truly want to express.

Some stories in the Bible explicitly demand this kind of appraisal. They are intentionally using language to say the unsayable. These stories I term "archetypal stories."

An archetypal story is a particular way of using words to express the inexpressible.

Perhaps an illustration would drive the point home. Boy meets girl. They fall in love. Boy takes girl out for dinner. Across the table as he holds her hands he gazes at her and says, "You are the most beautiful girl in the world." What should the girl do? Ask him for the results of his statistical survey? What age group of girls is he talking about? One race or all races? Is the girl to take his statement literally? Not if she loves him. She should hear his words as indicating a deeper truth. Her lover is making some sort of existential declaration of commitment. (There may be ulterior motives, but I do not want to go there.) The boy is speaking in archetypal terms. His use of an archetypal story expresses truth better than a literal expression of his feelings ever could.[9]

In this way we can see that an archetypal story, as we are using it, expresses something that is important and ultimate. Far from being a fabrication, an archetypal story indicates the totally true.

The Stories of Genesis 1–11 as Archetypal Stories.

In reading the stories of Genesis 1–11 we must ask ourselves: What questions about ultimate truth are these archetypal stories raising? And, following that, what answers do they supply?

Since we know that archetypal stories are being used to express something that language itself can only feel after, we must be prepared to find in these chapters surprisingly complex thoughts dressed in a simple guise, startling ideas masked as a familiar notion, and profound challenges encompassed within a strange story. The people these ancient stories originated with were not fools. People who think they have discovered a discrepancy within the Bible that somehow has escaped notice down through the ages are fooling only themselves.

Let's begin.

Creation (Genesis 1:1–2:4a)

The common preconception of these verses is that they tell the tale of how the world and cosmos came into being.

Because the passage lists Creation's "generations" as it were, it reads like a kind of genealogy. This understanding sets up an immediate confrontation with the scientific point of view—with astronomy, astrophysics, geology, biology, and even with historical common sense. Chronologies based on Old Testament accounts calculate that the world is only a few thousand years old. Science, on the other hand, reckons that the cosmos has been in place for billions of years. Fossils show that some form of life has existed on our planet for many millions of years. The common preconception of the creation story—that it explains how the world and cosmos actually came into being—drives a wedge between faith, on the one hand, and science and common sense on the other. The person of faith feels obliged to make a choice. This dilemma has led some poor souls to argue that evidence such as ancient fossils have been put there by God to "deceive" and to "test our faith." If this is so, we have to ask after the character of God. Is such a God consistent with the God we encounter throughout the bulk of scriptural testimony? If so, would you want to have anything to do with him?

This entire conflict is founded on sand and is a waste of time. It assumes that the fundamental question the passage seeks to answer is: *How did the world come into being?* (By the way, some scientists rightly object to the assertion that science can only ask "how" while religion deals with "why." True science, in pursuing "how" will inevitably have to confront "why" also.)

The conflict I am alluding to is not truly a conflict between religion and science. It is a conflict between *two types of religious outlooks* based on *two very different ways of reading the Bible*—one, the literal and, the other, the archetypal.

The literal mode of reading fails miserably to grasp the Bible's true nature. It reduces words and understanding to an elementary level, ignoring complexity and innuendo altogether. And, it creates problems for itself. For example, if light is created on the first day and there is no sun until the fourth day, what is the nature of that first day's light? And again, when we use the word "day" we are referring to the inter-relationship of the sun, the moon, and the earth. If there are no sun and moon until day four what is meant by dividing the period prior to their creation into three "days"? To argue that the creation process took six twenty-four-hour periods (six days) is not only in tension with science but with Genesis itself. To take the words at their face value is, as I hope to show, to miss the depths and the challenge of the passage as a whole. We are dealing with an archetypal story. Why is the entire passage structured into seven days in the first place? There is a reason. We will shortly discover it. For now, it is enough to observe that the intentional use of the word "day" says something otherwise unsayable.

There are so many interesting things to note. First, the Hebrew for God in this passage is not YHWH but *elohim,* the plural of *el.*[10] From what we learned earlier we might conclude that the passage therefore is an E passage. This would be wrong for we also learned that in Genesis J and P predominate. Are there indications that P's interest (the priestly, worship-centered interest) might be the main and controlling factor here? Keep this question in mind.

Second, notice the method of the creation process. Often it is said that in this passage we encounter the power of God's creating word, based on the model "God said and it was." But if we read carefully we will see that this dynamic of pure speaking applies only in the case of the creation of the first light. In all the other instances the pattern is "God said and God made and it was." Between the speaking and the being is the "making." Is there something in common about this making stage? Prompted by this question we can see that each act of creation is, in fact, *a separation* of this from that: waters below from waters above, sky from earth, dry land from seas, and so on. Indeed, the very first act of creation is imposed on something already there—the formless and empty deep. Order is separated from chaos. (The doctrine of *creatio ex nihilo*—"creation out of nothing"—evolved slowly and did not receive full articulation until the late second century CE. Whether it is implied by or compatible with the Genesis account is a debate amongst theologians and philosophers of science. It need not detain us more than to note that the full blown doctrine is not to be found in our passage.) The creation process takes the form of acts of separation. Created things become distinctive as they are separated from other created things. This is God's intention for his creation—that each created thing in it must be distinct and thus true to itself; that it must be the way God intends it to be.

Third, as we noted, the separation process is divided into a series of "days." Each day concludes with its work being pronounced "good" by God. (The interesting exception to this pattern is the omission of the verdict at the end of the second day, but this is balanced by a repetition on the third day.) And, to be good as we have seen is to be distinctively separated; to be uniquely what God intends.

And so, primarily, we have to see that God's overall creating action is not some powerful explosion of something out of nothing but the shaping of chaos and threat (the formless deep) into something "good." All this, of course, points to a higher range of meaning for the passage than a bald and literal description of how the world came into being. Furthermore, if this archetypal story proclaims that all creation is good we have to ask if we can possibly measure up to its challenge. Do we call "good" all that is to be found in creation—germs, sharks, avalanches, and so on? This ancient story has awesome courage. It affirms that *things are good if they are the way God wants them to be.* They may not be the way we want them to be, but that is our problem not creation's. Biblical ethics has to start here. And if we observe from an informed biblical perspective that something is not the way God intends it to be then what is the right thing to do? *To eradicate, or to empower it?* This question has profound implications and ought to color our ecclesiology and evangelism. More on this later.

With this clue we may move nearer to an understanding of the question the passage is seeking to answer.

The process of separation continues in the Genesis verses until it reaches a climax with the creation of humanity. Humanity is separated from all other created things, but the nature of its separation is highly distinctive. Humanity alone is created in God's "image." Humanity is the ultimately separated one. This separation carries with it a responsibility. Human distinctiveness is a task not a privilege. Humanity alone is given dominion over all creation, not for the sake of exploitation, but in order to be God's agent in and for creation. Our "image" embodies responsibility. We are created to fulfill a task—to love and care for creation. Humanity is called to be God in and for all creation.[11]

Additionally humanity receives a new and fresh word from the creator God—an imperative, a command. The first command in the Bible is, "Be fruitful and multiply." Humanity is to extend horizontally throughout creation and to expand its influence. Reproduction is part of the fulfillment of the task and responsibility of having dominion. This explains the inclusion of the genealogies. These documents with their odd lists seem so removed from us, but to the redactors they were evidence of the obedience to this first commandment. They are part and parcel of the story.

This is not all. On the seventh day God rests. It is hard to imagine how or why God Almighty would need to rest. The rest of God must be creative in some way, an active process, and part of the creative dynamic of separation. Humanity is summoned by his example to rest also, to mimic the creating rhythm of separation in daily and weekly living. The seventh day is to be separated from the other six. By resting in the Creator's world and when the Creator rests, humanity is living with God in a special way—in sacred space and time.

Through this examination of the passage we surely see now more clearly the hand and mind of P. You will remember we noted above that P represents the priestly strand of tradition. The P point of view is that worship and cultic observance lie at the heart of meaning and hope. For the priestly interest, the temple was the center of the universe and what went on in the temple was of ultimate and defining importance. The temple was for P the place and time of guaranteed sacred encounter. Thus for P *the heart of human nature* is worship. To worship is to intentionally put ourselves in sacred space and time. Humanity is the creature called to live in sacred space and time. That is what makes a human good.

Thus we hear the question this ancient archetypal story is trying to pose and then the answer it supplies. What makes life good? Put another way: What does it mean to be human? P answers:

- *To be human is to live in sacred space and time, and this kind of living empowers humanity to exercise dominion—to be God in and for all creation.*

Garden (Genesis 2–3)

In this passage we find what appears at first glance to be a second creation story. It is apparently quite different from the first archetypal story, but this need not trouble us. The redactors who put Genesis together could see as clearly as we can that the order of Creation in this story clashes with the first, that the male-to-female relationship is different, and that the acts of Creation themselves are not the same. The *presence* of these inconsistencies is not the issue; their *meaning* is. The question is not how to reconcile the two stories, but rather what is the nature of this second archetypal story? What *new* question is it posing and answering that the first did not address?

Immediately, we notice that God is described throughout these chapters as the "LORD God." The word "LORD" indicates the presence of the Hebrew YHWH, and so we can assume that this archetypal story is a J story. (We may want to note that since P was the redactor of material that already existed it follows that the P creation story is much more recent than this, J, story.) The J tradition, as we saw above, stems from the tribes who had actually experienced slavery in Egypt, the Exodus, the covenant, and the conquest of Canaan. These events naturally shaped the J compilers' theological understanding. God is personal in this tradition. He is referred to by name. We should expect—and certainly not be puzzled, alarmed, or surprised by—an emphasis and point of view quite different from P's in Genesis 1. Gone will be the focus on worship. Instead, we must look for themes of bondage, freedom, rescue, and intimate encounter.

Creation in the first story was by way of separation. Here, the creation process is taken up with names and being true to the name you are given. The male is named "Adam." This puns on the Hebrew word for "ground" or "earth" or "red." If we note the method of Adam's creation (God fashions a clay sculpture and then breathes into it the breath of life) we should call him "mud-man." In a sense we all are simply animated mud. Adam's name anticipates his fate at the end of the story. There, he is sentenced to work the ground, to pay with hard sweat for all he needs to nourish and sustain himself and his family. The redness of soil is echoed in his name after all, just as it must have stained his hands. Eve's name is like the Hebrew for "living" and it too fits the role she is given at the end of the story.[12] She is sentenced to pain but out of that pain will come the gift of new life.

This story is a series of encounters: of Adam with his loneliness, of Eve with the snake, of all three with the Lord God, and thus of all three with what they could have been and have, in fact, become. Recall our ethical question after the first creation story: if something is not the way God intends it to be then what is the right thing to do? To eradicate, or to empower it? What does God do here?

The account is told with a beguiling simplicity. The image of God walking in the garden to catch a little shade, of his needing to call out to Adam to find out where he is, of Adam blaming Eve and Eve blaming the snake: all these elements suggest a fairy tale or children's story. But this is no nursery rhyme. This narrative is dealing with matters that are deadly serious. Look at its guiding themes; gifts, obedience, responsibility, disregard, guilt, deception, and death. Underlying the charm is the profound assertion that all life is a gift of love from the Lord God whose only requirement is that we honor his parameters for us. This assertion is balanced by the claim that we flout God's requirement and disregard his gift. We pretend we have the right to do whatever we want. It is this, the human response to the wonders of the Garden, that leads to expulsion. But God's love is steadfast. Despite Adam and Eve's failure and despite the fact that they deserve to die, God shows mercy. He clothes them and gives them a second chance, albeit one that promises hardship.

What does God do? Here is our answer.

- *Mercy does not eradicate—it empowers.*

The theme of nakedness needs some attention. At the conclusion of Genesis 2 Adam and Eve are naked and feel no shame (Gen. 2:25). After they eat the fruit and God discovers their deception they are deeply ashamed of their nakedness (Gen. 3: 7 and 11). Why should this be? We must not apply our contemporary obsession with body image to this passage. Adam and Eve are man and wife. Whence the shame? The problem is not that they are naked and seen by each other, but that they are naked and thus are seen *in truth*. Adam is now seen as he truly is. It is not his physical nakedness but his psychological exposure that he can not stand. It is the same for Eve. Each sees self as a disobedient wretch—guilty, unthankful, and selfish. No wonder they try to cover up themselves with fig leaves.[13] They are no longer what God intends them to be. They have become a distortion of their true selves. As such they do not want to be seen.

What question, then, might this second archetypal story be asking? I suggest it is the question: Why is life so hard? Why is it such a struggle, so fraught with danger, pain, and hard work?

The answer in the story is clear. What causes all the struggle, pain, and hardship is our own misuse of freedom. Freedom is both a responsibility and risk. The Lord God did not place robots in the garden but beings capable of hearing, understanding, and responding—either in favor of the will of God or against it. God's command concerning the tree is absolute. He gives no explanation or apology. This throws human freedom into radical relief. As the Lord's will is clear and unambiguous so, too, must the response be. Humanity's response, however, falls short of the requirement and the "rest is history." History becomes a story of muck and madness, struggle and strife.

It is important to note that nowhere in this story does either of the following two words occur: "fall" and "sin." The archetypal story does not speak of human rebellion and its consequences. Paul will make such a reading almost normative for Christians through his exquisite and influential argument offered in Romans. But, his reading is not the natural reading of the story as it stands. It is not the intended "message" of J, and J's voice, for now, is what we are trying to hear. What J sadly seeks to explain is how and why life is so hard for us so much of the time. The tradition's answer is that we have chosen to be out of sync with the will of God. In spite of this, God shows tremendous love and mercy even while he expels humanity from the Garden, the place where he would have us live. Freedom is a risk. It accounts for the difficulty of living.

Brothers (Genesis 4)

Cain is a farmer and Abel is a shepherd. Many cultures have stories of tension between farmers and shepherds that echo the conflict we find here between Cain and Abel.

Stories that are told in the past tense to explain a present state of affairs or phenomenon are termed "etiological." An example of an etiology is the ancient Greek story of Typhon. It told of a monster called Typhon who was vanquished by the gods and thrown into the depths of the earth beneath Mount Etna. That mountain's occasional eruptions were attributed to the still-fuming anger of Typhon, trapped deep below.

In some sense the story of Cain and Abel is an etiology. It explains the tension between urban settled life and the nomadic free life of the "open range." We can see this problem worked out in the famous musical, *Oklahoma* and especially in the song, "The Farmer and the Cowman Should Be Friends." But, is etiology all there is to this story of the two brothers? By no means.

With our contemporary psychological proclivities we want explanations for the favor Abel enjoyed. Why was his sacrifice acceptable to God while Cain's was not? Just as there is no explanation or rationale offered with God's command not to eat from the tree of the knowledge of good and evil, so no explanation or rationale is offered here. Certainly, both animal and vegetable (grain, and so on) offerings were considered satisfactory later in Israel's history. The archetypal story does not concern itself with why at this time one sacrifice was pleasing and the other not. Its point lies elsewhere. (This illustrates the difference of the Bible from us culturally. Our culture is so imbued with psychology that we assume there must be some such explanation for the Cain-Abel conflict. The Bible's culture knows nothing of this avenue of reasoning.)

Note especially the important verse 4:7. God alerts Cain to the insidious, ever-present power of sin. This is *before* he kills Abel. It is the first mention of sin in the Bible. In some sense, Cain and Abel embody the real story of the Fall. Cain falls into sin; he gives in to the ensnaring power about which God himself has warned him.

Sin's terrible power lies in Cain's own desires, preferences, and decisions. Cain wants to assert himself over his brother and insinuate himself into his brother's place. The result is the death of Abel. The snake had promised Eve that she would not die, and she did not—at least not in the instant of her disobedience, which is the clear implication in the story. But now death comes, and it comes at the hand of another human being—a brother.

Cain, of course, is caught. Later, biblical laws concerning capital punishment would be established, but instead Cain is sentenced to live in the land of Nod, the Hebrew word for "wandering." His punishment (to live a nomadic life in contrast to the settled life of the farmer.) is more than he can bear. He rightly perceives that everyone will seek to kill him. More death. But God protects him by another act of mercy and love. He puts a mark on Cain's forehead. This mark of Cain—far from being a curse as many would have it—is a protecting sign, a mark that God is our champion.

- *Cain is empowered, not eradicated.*

The passage concludes with a vision of urban life. Cain, according to the story, becomes the father of the city, of technology, music, and the agriculture needed to support it all. (This archetypal thrust shows how small-minded the question "Where did Cain's wife come from?" really is. That question assumes Cain is meant to be understood literally—as the surviving son of the first two people on earth. Such a reading trivializes the story and fails to see its archetypal power.) We finish, however, with a chilling vision of pride in death, the curse of Lamech, in verses 23–24.

The theme of the entire story is death. Cain inflicts it then fears it, and Lamech boasts about causing it. What a distance we have moved from life in the Garden.

If we step back we can see that the archetypal story we have been looking at is wrestling with the question "What makes life bad?" Its answer is more than a simple blaming of human cruelty and stupidity. Cain disregards God's warning. He asserts self over all other interests. In doing this he embodies pride in human power—a human power that thinks it can get away with anything, do whatever it wants. The results are devastating. *What makes life bad is self-assertion over others. This is what sin is.* Individual sins are simply the actions motivated by this self-assertion.

Cain shows that humanity is in sin's grip. *His* is the story of the Fall. It is the story of death.

Flood (Genesis 6–9)

The saga of Noah is told so often to children it is hard to tune in to it with adult ears. Its dark tones have been painted over with the pastel hues of the nursery. What does the story tell us?

First, God is so disgusted with how the world has turned out that he decides to destroy all life. Read that sentence again. Death had been brought about by Cain and relished by Lamech. Now it will pour down from the sky. Here in the flood story God seems to decide to abandon empowerment as an ethical solution and give in to eradication.

The particular occasion for the Flood is given in 6:1–4. Here, we see a stark picture of sexual exploitation. Who the "sons of God" are is uncertain, but they seem to be related in some way to the "Nephilim" and the "heroes of old." In medieval Europe the feudal lord had *ius prima noctis,* the "right of the first night," with any peasant bride on his land. The setting of this biblical passage is much the same. The problem is not promiscuity as such. Rather, it is the way the stronger makes use of the weaker. Power wrongly exercised (the radical assertion of self) emerges as a theme again, just as it did in Cain's story.

Second, and in particular, humanity is singled out as being thoroughly bad and deserving of death. Read Genesis 6:5 and note in particular the qualifiers, "every," "only," "all the time." There is no wiggle room here. Humankind is totally depraved. (John Calvin did not invent the notion of total depravity.) Noah is regarded as "righteous" but only in comparison with those of his "generation." He is the best of a totally bad lot.

Third, the structure of the ark is detailed. It makes for a dismal environment. One tiny window (eighteen inches is the traditional "cubit," the distance from the elbow to the fingertips) is placed at the top. Only one window. And, it is not a real boat either as there is no means of propulsion or steering. The ark is like a raft with sides and a roof. In fact, it is more like a floating tomb than anything else. After one year the window is finally opened again—after one year, trapped inside with all those animals and in-laws. (For the length of the flood compare verses 7:11 and 8:13.) Into that tomb had gone all of life—but out it came again.

Fourth, the Flood does not change humankind. Compare 8:21 with 6:5. The Flood does change something, though. For the first time in the Bible the notion of "covenant" is introduced. *What the Flood changes is not humankind but the relationship between God and the world.* This change results in God establishing a covenant with humanity.

A covenant is not a contract, made between two equal partners and involving differing but balanced responsibilities. A covenant is the deal made between a conqueror and those whom he has beaten. What it says, in effect is: "I will protect you in the future, but this is what you must do for me." Those at the receiving end have no real choice. In this case God is the conqueror; he has rescued humankind from the Flood. They are in no position to bargain.

If we read the passage carefully we will see there are etiological elements in this flood story. It accounts for the eating of meat, the variety of human races, the ancient memory of a great flood, and the tension with Canaanites. The overriding interest of the archetypal story, however, is its conclusion—namely the establishment of the covenant, of a new relationship between God and humankind.

Given the prevalence of violence (radical self-assertion) amongst all cultures, the question the archetypal story is wrestling with is this: What will make life possible? Its answer is the covenant. Life must be lived under the conditions God establishes, otherwise death will triumph. In turn, God promises there will be no more eradication.

- *God's way with humankind will be empowerment, and the covenant serves to enshrine this promise as an institutional formality.*

Tower (Genesis 11:1–9)

Clearly, etiological elements continue to linger in the tower story as well. To understand this it is important to know a little about the ancient city of Babylon. This cosmopolitan city constituted one of the major focal points of world power in the ancient Middle East. (See Figure 1 in the appendix.) During the biblical period, from 2000 BCE until the advent of Persian power in the early sixth century BCE, Assyria and then Babylon were the only competitors to Egyptian might. During the height of Babylon's power it conquered Israel, destroyed the temple, and exiled the people. We will be focusing a great deal of our attention on Babylon below as we examine the trauma of this event for Israel. It is enough to say for now that Babylon, in Hebrew eyes, was a potent symbol of human haughtiness and self-confidence. The ancient city of Babylon had a style of stepped pyramids, called ziggurats, the remains and ruins of which have been excavated in modern times. The tower story seeks to account for these structures and for Babylonian pride. Also, the story attempts to explain the world's obvious linguistic variety. This etiological dimension, however, does not address the archetypal elements of the story.

The key to the archetypal story is carried by the thrice-repeated use of the word "scattered." Note its occurrences. The tower builders seek to avoid being "scattered," and God brings it about. Being scattered is what humanity avoids and God wills. Humanity wills unity—to be settled in one place, working on one project, communicating in one language. The tower is in a city, a place of coming together. Once again we encounter here a negative evaluation of city life. (This negativity is balanced later in the Old Testament. Through the P and D traditions Jerusalem rises to pre-eminence, and this theme is picked up again at the end of Revelation.) Just as it was in the story of Cain and the story of the generation of Noah, the sub-theme here is self-assertion—the imposition of human will over and against the will of God. The tower is built higher and ever higher, until it reaches into the heavens—God's space. Later Jewish legend will tell of archers climbing to the top of the tower and shooting their arrows into the sky in the hopes of wounding the gods.

The question this archetypal story asks is clear: Can life ever be good again? What could possibly be better than getting all people together—working together on one common project, speaking one common language? The tower building is a parable of human togetherness, building a better world for our children and grandchildren. The story reads like a political slogan. Together we can build a good life again. Get together. Join up. We can do it. But human cooperation without God will always be a dismal failure. So, can life ever be good again? What is unclear (to me at any rate) is if the story, in posing this question, manages in any way to give us an answer. God keeps his promise to Noah. He does not give in to eradication, but at the same time it is hard to see the scattering of the people as an empowerment. The ending is ambiguous. Its open-endedness pours us forward towards Genesis 12 and, indeed, the rest of the biblical account.

- *How will this eradication-empowerment struggle be resolved? The answer lies ahead.*

Summary

The Genesis stories have posed questions that lie at the center of our lives.

- What makes life good, and what is the real heart of human nature? (Creation)

- Why is life so hard? (Garden)

- What makes life bad? (Brothers)

- How is life possible? (Flood)

- Can life be good again? (Tower)

The questions are profound. Beneath them there is a certainty—that God wills what is good. But how will God's good prevail in our lives? And so, the answers these ancient stories (archetypal stories) provide make us long for something more. They lead us to the edge of expectancy. Like the generation of the Tower-builders, we are left drifting, scattered, and uncertain.

We need help. We need empowering help. Where, how, from whom is the help to come and what will it be like?

This is the question the rest of Bible is written to answer.

3

History: An Answer to the "Help-We-Need"

❖

(Genesis 12:1–9; Exodus 3 and 14:5–31; Deuteronomy 7:1–9; Judges 13–16; 1 Samuel 8; 2 Samuel 5:1–7; 1 Kings 12:1–24)

(See the appendix *Idiot Sentences One, Two, and Three* and the corresponding *Patterns of Geschichte* diagrams, Figures 7-11.)

Two Views of History

The Germans have two words that we can translate with our word "history."

The first is *Historie* and it means "what actually happened." Most of us are inclined to think that this is what history is; the study of what actually happened. History, sadly, is far more complex than that.

Consider the assassination of President John F. Kennedy. There is still a great deal of debate, even decades after the event, about what actually happened. Some people are sure that there was one shooter while others conclude that the evidence proves this to be impossible. Some people blame the CIA, Lyndon Johnson, the Mob, even Fidel Castro and say there is a bizarre and hugely successful secret conspiracy behind the event. We simply cannot know the truth for certain.

Or consider an example from classical history that had a lasting impact on Christianity—the battle of the Milvian Bride in 312 CE. On the death of the Roman emperor a civil war broke out between rival generals, each seeking the imperial power. One of these generals was a man named Constantine. At the Milvian Bridge the two armies gathered for a decisive battle. It is claimed that Constantine, the night before the conflict, had seen a cross in the night sky and heard the words, "In this sign conquer." Accordingly, the next morning he adorned his soldiers' shields with this emblem and was victorious. His success led him to establish Christianity as the religion of the Roman Empire, and this in turn led to the creation of Christendom. Did this astronomical oddity actually happen, or was it a later spin of some ideological kind?

Our inability to be certain about historical events is due precisely to the reality represented in the other German word for history, *Geschichte. Geschichte* is "the meaning of what happened."

John F. Kennedy was murdered. That literally happened. In addition, however some see this event as bringing to an end the era of optimism and boundless progress that had preceded it. They believe it lay to rest the modern era while ushering in a time of post-modernity. There was more at stake than the death of a single man. So with Constantine. Whatever actually happened, the victory at the Milvian Bridge that day in 312 CE led to the Christianization of the Roman Empire. Whether this was a good thing or a bad thing has been variously debated by historians, some seeing it as ushering in the dawn of a new day for Europe and others seeing it as the beginning of the end of classical civilization. Whatever the truth may be, a great deal of meaning and interpretation has accompanied the recorded event.

Modern science teaches us that observers alter and condition to some extent what they observe. There has long existed a debate as to whether light is made up of waves or particles. If experiments are set up to look for light waves then that is what is observed. Equally, if experiments are established to look for particles, lo and behold particles are discovered. The observation process itself in some weird way impacts what is being observed. It is not a case of what-you-see-is-what-you-get but of what-you-look-for-is-what-you-get.

History is not immune to this. In some sense all written history is *Geschichte.*[14] Even when historians have the clearest intentions to write what actually happened they cannot help but explain things a little to let the reader see something of the meaning behind the facts. Many attorneys know that eyewitnesses provide the most unreliable while at the same time the most persuasive type of evidence. When we read history we must not simplistically assume that we are reading what actually happened, even when the account sounds like eyewitness evidence. With history, as with the light as wave or particle controversy, often what you look for is what you get.

History as the "Help-We-Need"

In the last chapter we discovered that the overriding question Genesis leaves us with is: Where we will find the "help-we-need?" By this hyphenated phrase, the help-we-need, I mean to indicate the human condition at the end of Genesis 1–11. By the end of our review of the five fundamental questions of life we saw that we needed help. This help is needed to allow us to be what we are meant to be, God's special creatures separated from others to live in sacred space and time and care for all creation. So again; where will we find the-help-we-need? We saw that Genesis is "the midst" for the rest of the Bible. We can expect, therefore, to find voices addressing this difficult dilemma as we read further into the Bible.

The first answering voice is biblical history itself. Is that voice *Historie* or *Geschichte*? Luckily, we have strong clues from within the text.

As we shall see below in some detail, the Jews divide their Scriptures into three sections, the second of which they call *Neviim*, meaning "prophets." This section includes the following separate books: Joshua, Judges, Samuel, and Kings. I am sure few if any readers will have thought of these books as anything other than historical, as books of *Historie*. They tell of heroes and military events, settlements, and the socio-economic and cultural development of Israel. They read like history books and yet, despite their apparent content, they are regarded by Jews as "prophecy." Why? By referring to them this way the Jewish tradition declares that these books are *Gechichte*. They give us the meaning behind the events they describe.

For example, Joshua paints a picture of a blitzkrieg conquest of the Promised Land, while Judges tells of slow infiltration. What actually happened: blitzkrieg or slow infiltration; neither or a combination? Was it perhaps in the interest of Joshua to paint a picture of a hugely successful single military campaign, one that took place under his leadership, after all? Was it not equally in the interests of the individual tribes to tout the role of their various champions in defeating the enemy over a long period and in many locales, as recounted in Judges? In giving these differing points of view, Joshua and Judges are in fact presenting their interpretation of the meaning of what happened.

Another clue comes from the pages of some of the books of Joshua, Judges, Samuel, and Kings themselves. Several times we come across a verse such as 1 Kings 14:19: "The other events of Jeroboam's reign, how he fought and how he ruled, are recorded in the Annals of the Kings of Israel." That is to say, the reader is being told: If you want *Historie* go read elsewhere.

Another example: Scholars know, as a historical fact, what an influential and long-serving king Omri, King of Israel was. Their knowledge is based on records external to the Bible. Yet the biblical account dismisses this significant ruler in a few short verses and then summarizes in 1 Kings 16:27: "The other events of Omri's reign, [and] his actions, and the exploits he performed, are recorded in the Annals of the Kings of Israel." Clearly, the estimation of Omri in Kings, that he was of little consequence because he neglected to serve God, is made on the basis of the meaning of his reign. This is a *Geschichte* judgment. If you want *Historie* read elsewhere—in the Annals of the Kings of Israel.

Many more examples could be given to establish this fundamental point. It is worth repeating:

- *History in the Bible is Geschichte—history as meaning, as an answer to the "help-we-need." As such it is a response to the deepest cry of the human spirit.*

If you assume biblical history is *Historie* you will conclude it is bad history. If, however, you understand it to be what it is, *Geschichte*, then you will be prompted to ask about meaning, significance, and its impact for your own life.

Meaning as Contest

Our readings will reveal that the meaning of the biblical *Geschichte* is couched in terms of a contest between the will of God, on the one hand, and the ways of the world, on the other.

It is very important to remember that in the Genesis account of Creation God's opinion of the world, of physical reality, is that it is "good, very good." The idea that physicality *per se* is corrupting is not a Hebrew view. This view, of course, is found elsewhere, for example, in the philosophy of ancient Greece. Other religious traditions believe that life in this world is either an illusion (Hinduism) or merely a cause of suffering (Buddhism.) The biblical witness is very different from this. The Bible testifies to the goodness of life, of the world, and of physical existence. The problems the Bible seeks to account for are not physical but moral, emotional, and spiritual—all based on human willfulness. There is nothing wrong with the world as such; there is everything wrong with the human attitudes to the world, to life, to one another, and to God. As we have seen, this is the issue Genesis articulates in its great archetypal stories. This why we need help.

Having said all that, however, the Bible frankly acknowledges that the world is an arena where there is a latent lure. Its latency is exactly what the serpent in the Adam and Eve archetypal story represents. The voice of this lure is not that of a talking snake but of a chattering, wooing, noisy world. It tempts us to think that the world is all there is and that it alone ought to be the measure of meaning, value, and purpose. The "ways of the world" can easily make us forget God and reject our calling. The result of this forgetting is what is meant by the term "sin." Sin is the condition of having forgotten what a human being truly is—a creature uniquely made to live in God's image and summoned to live in sacred space and time. And, as we have noticed earlier, the primary and most obvious manifestation of sin is the radical assertion of self as the meaning of life. The ways of the world are the cumulative pressure to ignore our calling and neglect our mission.[15]

Thus, if God is to give us the "help-we-need" to remember, recover, and revitalize this calling and mission, it clearly follows that his help-giving will in some sense be in conflict with the ways of the world. Traditional language describes this contest as a battle between grace and sin.[16] This archetypal struggle runs throughout the Bible from Creation on. We see an increasing encroachment into God's good creation by the world—and a narrowing of the zone of God's influence. (See Figure 12 in the appendix.)

Some religions base their theology on the idea of these two warring tendencies. They believe a great cosmic struggle actually exists between the power of good (God) and the power of evil (the Devil). This idea can be found in the context of ancient Israel's developing faith system, and echoes of it are heard from time to time throughout the Bible. A stunning biblical text, however, highlights ancient Israel's ultimate rejection of this dualism. Isaiah 45:7 states: "I form light and create darkness, I make weal and create woe—I the LORD do all these things." Behind the great struggle of good and evil lies the will of the one God. This is a hard teaching. Perhaps the hardest part is that it locates the problem, not on some far-away cosmic battlefield, but squarely in the center of the human predicament.

We can summarize all this by saying that *Geschichte* in the Bible is played out in the conflict between two human relationships; our relationship with the world and our relationship with God. The struggle is, in fact, our struggle to become truly human. Thus, the greatest conflict of all is located in the depths of the human heart.[17]

More Than a Timeline.

We all are familiar with a history timeline in which events and people are placed one after the other in chronological order. Biblical events, as we noted earlier, stretch from 2000 BCE to about 100 CE. Using these dates as the beginning and end of a timeline we could easily place the Bible stories in sequential order.

This data would miss, however, the aspect of history we are most interested in—that is, how it offers us the "help-we-need." In order to see the *Historie* as *Geschichte*, we need to add another dimension to the timeline, a dimension indicating value of some kind. In our case the value is getting closer to the will of God and the negative is drifting towards the ways of the world. This value can be represented by a plus sign and a minus sign. As history realizes the value it will pull the line upwards towards the plus sign. The opposite trend indicates a drifting from the value.

For our purposes, this value-added dimension indicates whether certain biblical events and the people involved in them are getting closer or farther away from realizing God's purpose. Some events sweep human affairs up into the plus sign territory (towards manifesting the "help-we-need") while others drag human affairs down into the minus-sign zone. (See the various illustrations of *Patterns of Geschichte* in the appendix using this concept, Figures 7-11.)

As we progress through biblical history searching for the "help-we-need," we will be able to add events and people to this value-tilted timeline. By the end we will be able see an archetypal pattern to biblical history.

Genesis 12:1–9: Call, Promise, and Wandering

The passage of supreme significance for understanding biblical history as answer to the "help-we-need" is Genesis 12:1–3:

> The LORD said to Abram, "Go forth from your native land and from your father's house to the land that I will show you. I will make of you a great nation, and I will bless you; I will make your name great, and you shall be a blessing. I will bless those who bless you, and curse him that curses you; and all the families of the earth shall bless themselves by you.

This passage starts *Geschichte*. It provides context without which all history would remain just one thing happening after another. Here the archetypal pattern is established.

Notice first to whom God is speaking. It is not "Abraham" but "Abram." Hebrew names have meanings. *Ab* is the Hebrew for "father," and *ram* is the Hebrew for "mighty." God begins the march of biblical history by talking to Big Daddy. The passage goes on to tell us why this man is Big Daddy. He is rich and powerful, a chief, a patriarch. Abram is the strongest force around. Wealth and power—what more does anyone need? By the world's measure of success he truly is Big Daddy.

There are, however, two holes in the heart of this portrait of success. Big Daddy has no land of his own. He is a semi-nomadic wanderer. He has no place he can call home; no earth to sink his hands into. He must forever wander on the edges of stability. More than this, he has no son, no heir, no hope of being remembered, and therefore to his mind, no real future. (The lack of a son as distinct from the lack of a child is part of the patriarchalism of biblical culture. See note 7.)

So it is that God speaks to Big Daddy and promises him a land of his own and, by implication, a son. Abram is promised that his descendants will be a "great nation." Later he is told that they will be as numerous as the grains of sand on the shore or the stars in the sky. Why does God do this? Just to be nice or to take pity on a childless old man? No, God has a very specific purpose in mind. Reread Genesis 12:1–3.

All peoples are to be blessed. *Everyone* is to be helped.

The "help-we-need" is going to come to the world through Big Daddy's people. God renames Big Daddy, changing his name from Abram to Abraham, which means "father of the people." Which people? The people who bring to the world ("all the families of the earth") the "help-we-need." This is the Bible's fundamental and controlling dynamic. (See Figure 6 in the appendix.)

This is an astonishing passage. If you memorize no other verses from the Bible memorize Genesis 12: 1–3. They are the key to unlock the meaning of the Bible as a whole. Behind this story is a premise, without which the entire thing makes no sense. The premise of this promise to Big Daddy is that God cares about the world.

The foundation for this Abrahamic enterprise is God's love for us. Because God loves the world he seeks to give it the help it so desperately needs. Everything else in the Bible flows from this. Indeed, the entire Bible can be summed up in this one insight: God always seeks to save us.

Moreover, the passage makes an assertion. The "help-we-need" is going to come through the story of a people. God has chosen the messy realities of this people's development, loyalty, and faithfulness as his means for helping the world. There will be no legions of angels pouring down from heaven to sweep opposition aside and encourage the troops. There will be no overwhelming demonstrations of power and no cosmic reversal. Instead, there will be a story—a people's story, one imbued with meaning and purpose. And that is how God is going to give us the "help-we-need."

History has begun, both *Historie* and with it *Geschichte*, through the fact that Big Daddy has been given a call and a promise. History has a purpose, to give all peoples the "help-we-need"—help that the human spirit cries out for at the end of Genesis 1–11; help to realize the image of God, to live in sacred space and time caring for all creation and enabling it to become "good, very good" once again. This story is a mighty reaffirmation of God's option for empowerment over eradication.

The story of Abraham adds value to history's timeline by providing a clear method for calculating history's progress. What must be traced is the history of his descendents, but history as more than that people's *Historie*. Will that history show and offer all people the "help-we-need," or will it hide and hinder it? Will Abraham's people embody *Geschichte* as they were called to do?

Abraham hears God's call and promise, and he is faithful to them. Abandoning his ancestral nomadic areas in Mesopotamia (again see Figure 1 in the appendix) he obediently travels east until he arrives in the Promised Land. Genesis 12:5–6 summarizes an ominous and indelible reality for those who descend, literally and spiritually, from Abraham, for those who inherit the call and promise to him. The verses read, "When they arrived in the land of Canaan…the Canaanites were then in the land."

The Promised Land was not empty. Not only was it inhabited, but those who were there were settled in. They were an agricultural, military, urban, and highly civilized nation. Archaeological scholarship has shown what a sophisticated people these Canaanites were. Abraham and his band of seminomadic shepherds must have seemed weak and insignificant in comparison. Through the archaeological discovery of an ancient library (at Mari) a term was found that referred to a class of people. The word is the Semitic word *hapiru,* and it is thought by scholars to designate any wandering semi-nomadic peoples who lived on the edges of civilization. It had a socio-economic, not a racial, connotation. Some scholars, but by no means all, think that the word "Hebrew" derives from *hapiru* and that Abraham and his people were regarded as marginal, unsophisticated, and lower class.

It is hard to think of a people today who have remained in the same place since the beginning of time. The displacement and migration of populations has been a global pattern for as long as humans have walked the earth. The history of Great Britain, for example, is a centuries' long story of wave after wave of new conquest and new conquerors.

So it is with Abraham and the Promised Land. The promise of Canaan to Abraham and his descendants is not made to legitimize the driving out of the Canaanites. Rather it emphasizes that the promise of the "help-we need" must be realized in the midst of and for all peoples. The working out of the biblical story will always involve interaction with others. That interaction is a key element in the entire program of God's plan for giving help. The purpose of the call to Big Daddy, after all, is to help "all" people. That "the Canaanite was then in the land" is not by accident. It provides Abraham's people with an opportunity and challenge. They are to work out their purpose in the context of other peoples. After all, God's plan is to impact the world. God's concern is not with Abraham and his people. They are a means to an end. The end is the restoration of all humanity to the full potential of living as God's image in sacred space and time.

We are thus clearly shown that to be chosen by God is to be chosen, not for privilege, but for responsibility. It is worth noting here that the dynamic tension between these two understandings of chosen-ness has colored the self-understanding of God's people ever since. It has plagued the Christian community in its debates over the meaning of "predestination," for example. It bears repetition:

- *the result of being chosen by God is not privilege but responsibility; not the giving of a reward but a summons to a task.*

The Canaanites are merely the first in a series of "foreign" nations in the Bible—that is, nations who are brought into collision with God's people and who thus represent the world that God wants to help. These foreign peoples play a major role in determining the pattern of history. The interaction of God's people with them is crucial in showing whether the value-added timeline which is *Geschichte* is proceeding positively or negatively.

The many foreign peoples mentioned in the Bible, eight are central, represent the "world" that "God so loved," and continues to love. Without them there is no *Geschichte*, only *Historie*. (See the appendix *Idiot Sentence One*.)

Meanwhile—back to the Canaanites. The presence of the Canaanites in the Promised Land is a problem that continues through the narratives of Abraham's son, Isaac, and his grandson, Jacob. Neither of them is able to set permanent roots down in the land. Their lives continue the pattern of wandering, of the unstable rootlessness that we first encountered when we met Big Daddy himself. They, too, are probably *hapiru*. And then Genesis embarks on the story of Joseph, Jacob's son.

The Joseph story is one of the world's great works of literature. It is like a novella, recounting as it does a tale of sibling rivalry, of inter-generational deception, and all leading to a cathartic reunion in the end. Yet, a theological and *Geschichte* crisis is packaged in this wonderful story. The fact that by the end of the book of Genesis Joseph has brought all his family, including Jacob, down to live in Egypt raises an intriguing question about God and the "help-we-need." Is the world, as represented by Egypt, a better home for God's people than the Promised Land? If the Canaanites remain in the land and God's people have withdrawn, what of the original intent of God's promise to Big Daddy? Has God somehow changed his mind? Is another plan unfolding?

This question only becomes apparent as the story continues in the opening verses of Exodus. We are stuck with a horrifying and stark reality. Joseph's descendants—brought by him to Egypt to receive bread and all that nourishes life in the face of famine—have ended up enslaved. Exodus poignantly and point-edly observes that "A new king arose over Egypt who did not know Joseph" (Exodus. 1:8). This does not mean that he lacks personal knowledge of the man. What it means is that enough time has passed that Joseph's role in saving Egypt from starvation has long since been forgotten. The new king, in looking out on his realm, has seen a large foreign population in his country and has decided to enslave them to meet his labor shortage. It all makes perfect sense—to him but not for us. From our point of view, slaves hardly present a promising formula or a credible force for bringing help to the world. Indeed, the world seems to have captured not only God's people but God's plan.

Exodus 3 and 14: 5–31: Slavery and Exodus

Moses towers over the story of God's people in the Hebrew Scriptures. Exodus 3 is pivotal in unlocking the force of his personality and the role he plays in the history we are reading about.

The Egyptians have become concerned about the over-breeding of their slave population. To remedy this problem Pharaoh has ordered the slaughter of all male newborn children. Baby Moses, born to a Jewish slave, is set afloat in a small basket to escape death. (Is this an Ark echo?) He is rescued by Pharaoh's daughter and from this time forward is brought up in the palace and corridors of power. Though he is raised as an Egyptian he is nevertheless aware of his origins. (The story tells us his birth mother becomes his nurse.) As a young adult Moses witnesses an Egyptian officer beating a slave, and in anger Moses strikes back and kills the Egyptian. When, later, he learns that this desperate act has become known he flees from Egypt to the desert country of the Sinai. There he settles down, marries, and spends what we are told is forty years of married life working as a shepherd for his father-in-law.

This is the context for our reading from Exodus 3. Consider these facts:

- Moses has abandoned his, and God's, people, leaving them enslaved by the world.

- Moses is a cop-killer.

- Moses has got away with murder.

- Moses has forged a new life for himself.

- Moses is no longer a young man.

All of this spotlights how unlikely a candidate Moses is as liberator. (We will encounter this principle throughout the Bible. God's choices are rarely based on worldly concepts of qualification.[18] God is the Lord of the imaginative choice.) Yet, by the end of the chapter, Moses is on his way back to Egypt. To do what? To free the slaves, of course.

Think about that from Pharaoh's point of view. What are slaves? They represent a guaranteed workforce, certain economic stability, and a permanent structure upon which to base social principles. From this point of view, then, ask yourself what Moses' mission really is. Moses is sent to destroy Egypt's economy, to upset the social order, and to instill uncertainty. No wonder this cop-killer is reluctant to accept the mission.

He makes all kinds of excuses. Surely, he suggests, God could find a better candidate. His most probing objection comes in the form of a theological puzzle. Reread Exodus 3:13–15. Moses knows he will be asked on what authority, in the name of what God, he is encouraging the slaves to revolt, to risk being slaughtered in anger—for that is what his mission entails from the slaves' point of view. The crucial connection is made in verse 16 when he is instructed to tell them that the God of his mission is the God of their fathers, the God of Abraham, the God of Isaac, and the God of Jacob.[19] The freedom on offer is an extension of God's plan. The escape from Egypt is part of the call and promise to Big Daddy. (The beat goes on. The archetypal pattern is about to swing back up from the minus zone.) But this is not enough for the cop-killer. He wants more information. He asks God what his name is.

In the ancient world, it was thought that the name of a thing represented that thing's essence. When Adam names a creature he somehow identifies through articulation that creature's essence. The name is what makes that creature distinct from all others. Adam's role as the one-who-names in the second creation story of Genesis echoes the way God creates by separating one thing from another in the first account. To know the name of a thing, therefore, is to have special knowledge and some degree of control over it. For this reason the God of the fathers is reluctant to disclose his name to Moses.[20]

So, when Moses asks God to tell him his name God's answer is wildly ambig-uous. Normally translated as "I am who I am," it amounts to a rebuke. It is as if God is saying to Moses: "You want to know my name, to understand my essence? Well, I say to you, mind your own business. I am who I am."[21]

But, there is even more to it than this. When we unpack the Hebrew of this name a whole range of meaning explodes out of it. The Hebrew phrase in Exodus 3:14, normally translated "I am who I am," is *ehyeh asher ehyeh*. Let's see what these Hebrew words mean.

First, *asher*. This is an all-purpose particle of relation. It is the equivalent of the English letters "wh-." This, of course, is wildly unhelpful in itself. The sense of the "wh-" has to be determined from the sentence in which it is placed. *Asher* can be translated "where, whence, whither, who, whom, whose, when, or why." Clearly, in our case, it cannot be translated at all until the meaning of rest of the sentence is confirmed.

Second, *ehyeh*. This is a form of the Hebrew verb "to be." Anyone who has ever studied a foreign language knows that the verb "to be" is always irregular, and so it is with Hebrew. Moreover, even the regular Hebrew verb does not oper-ate the way we would expect from our knowledge of European languages. Although the Hebrew verb does have a singular and plural for the first, second, and third persons, it has no tenses as such—no past, present, or future. Instead, the Hebrew verb is found in five forms and seven stems. Each of these forms and stems, in combination especially, changes the nuance of the verb's meaning. For example, one stem suggests reflexive action (doing something to or for self) while another connotes passive action (something is done to self.) The form of the verb "to be" that we encounter in this verse is first person, singular, and in the inten-sive stem.

Intensive. How can we translate the verb "to be" in an intensive way?

Let me illustrate the intensive stem by using the basic verb for "to touch." I could say in the basic stem "I touch you." But, if I were to use the intensive form of the same verb it would amount to saying "I hit you. I really touch you—hard."

How does this intensive sense work with the verb "to be"? What is the differ-ence in meaning between "I am" and "I really am?" You *are* sitting reading this book. Now, *intensively* be there reading the book. The reading stays the same. What can this possibly mean?

We are given a strong hint in Exodus 3:12 when God, in reply to Moses' hesi-tancy to undertake the task, says to him, "I will be with you." God recognizes the difficulty of what he is asking and acknowledges that Moses cannot be expected to complete the task on his own. Can this help us with *ehyeh asher ehyeh* and the need to translate those *ehyehs* intensively?

Remember the context. This conversation (a) is happening on a mountain many miles from Egypt in the land of the Kenites, (b) is sending Moses on a mission to leave and return to Egypt, and (c) has already covered the fact that Moses will need God's help. There are two obvious pairs of contrasts: first, between *here*, on this mountain, and *there*, in the land of Egypt; and second, between God, the commander, and Moses, the recruit. These two pairs of contrasting realities in the context of Exodus 3 throw some light, I believe, on how the name of God is best translated. When God says his name is *ehyeh asher ehyeh* he is in fact saying: I, here on this mountain with you, the one who is asking you to do this difficult thing, will be there, back in Egypt, helping you in the doing of it.[22]

I am here as the one who will be there.

This is the name of God.

This is the essence of what he will reveal to us of his nature. The rest remains hidden from us. But we need no more than this. This is who God is for us. God is the one who says, "I am here as the one who will be there."

- *The mode of God's presence is a promise of his future power.*

(We hear this same truth in the Christian Scriptures, in Romans 8:38–39: "For I am sure that neither death, nor life, nor angels, nor principalities, nor things present, nor things to come, nor powers, nor height, nor depth, nor anything else in all creation, will be able to separate us from the love of God in Christ Jesus our Lord.")

This name of God proclaims a powerful biblical principle that extends throughout the pages of both the Hebrew and Christian Scriptures. We must call it the incarnation principle. This principle makes a promise:

- *God will make the power of the "help-we-need" present in and for all life.*

This principle also tells us something about God:

- *God is the source of the "help-we-need."*

God will keep his promise to empower rather than eradicate—his name assures us of this.

The rest of the Exodus story is well known. Though Pharaoh is at first reluctant to let the people go, he finally buckles under the mounting pressure of the plagues (God's power made present.) Moses leads the people out of bondage—the world cannot keep God's people enslaved or God's plan in check for-ever. Not surprisingly, Pharaoh changes his mind at the last moment. The subsequent escape of the Hebrew people from his pursuing armies at the Red Sea only underscores the grace dimension of the narrative. The prophets would later speak of the Exodus event as a deliverance *by God*, mentioning Moses a mere five times (Is. 63:11, 12; Jer. 15:1; Mic. 6:4, and Mal. 4:4).

(And so we can see that through the Exodus event the archetypal movement [or *Geschichte* pattern] has returned to plus territory, following the dip into minus during the enslavement. Things are going well once again.)

Deuteronomy 7:1–9: Wilderness and Covenant

Freed from Egypt the people head out into the wilderness. But they do not go straight back to the land promised to Abraham. A generation perishes during the years between slavery and entering the Promised Land. Moses himself dies on Mount Nebo only catching a glimpse of the goal. Scholars debate the reasons for this delay. They point to the Israelite's constant complaining in the desert, their recurring longing to return to Egypt, their decision to worship a golden calf—all of which adds up to a severe case of feet-dragging. Whatever the explanation for the delay its consequence is clear. The delay allows the people to visit the holy mountain of Sinai. There they enter into a new covenant with God. We shall return below to some of the details of this covenant (the Ten Commandments, for example) but for now we shall simply note its impact, remembering always the dynamic of covenant as distinct from contract, as we noted above when we examined the Flood story.

The verses of our reading from Deuteronomy make this impact clear. The people, because they feel gratitude for their liberation are newly obliged to God. They are to undertake a radical new kind of "holiness." But all this is couched in the context of a disturbing new attitude to the world. Anticipating a return to the Promised Land the people envision a conquest, not an infiltration. The Canaan-ites are allied with six other national entities. These seven together are recognized in the text as strong and mighty, but with God's help their utter destruction is inevitable. The seven are to be destroyed and isolated. Intermarriage with them is to be an abomination. Racial and ethnic purity is to be maintained. Accompany-ing the return to the Promised Land there will be an act of ethnic cleansing. The very same divine power that visited the plagues on Egypt in the name of freedom now will be used to obliterate other people. The incarnation principle is being used here as an instrument of terror.

All this is given (as is most of Deuteronomy) in a speech from Moses, under God's command, to the people. These verses, therefore, reflect an understanding of God and God's will that strikes us as, at least in some measure, in tension with Genesis 12: 1–3. It is hard to see how, if you were one of the seven nations spoken of here, Abraham's people are going to be a blessing for you in any sense. It seems that eradication has swept empowerment aside.

What are we to make of all this? Several points must be noted.

First, there is a lot of morally reprehensible material in the Bible. The Bible itself is uneven. Not all parts or passages have to be taken with the same seriousness as every other. (We shall touch on thus more fully below in chapter 14, "Looking Ahead," when we examine the biblical tones of voice.)

Second, the picture of God in the Bible is uneven. In many places God sounds impish, devious, disputatious, and downright unlikable. He is made to sound that way by impish, devious, disputatious, and downright unlikable people.

Because of this we must always read the Bible with the five realities and three rules in mind. (And if you can't remember what they are, look back to Chapter One to remind yourself.) When these are coupled with all that we learned about *Historie* and *Geschichte*, we can often sift a great deal of sense out of passages that strike us, at first, as unworthy of attention.

So, it is here with our Deuteronomy verses. Two positive points can be taken from this otherwise disturbing passage.

* The concept of the holy.

One major consequence of the covenant made on Sinai is that the Israelites begin to see themselves as "holy." The Hebrew word for "holy," *qadosh*, and the Greek word for "holy," *hagios*, both mean the same thing. They mean "different, apart, and separate." To be holy is not to be better than, purer than, or more spiritual than the other. It is to be essentially different. This passage makes it clear that this difference lies in the nature of *what God wants to do* with his holy people and what he *wants them to do*. It has nothing to do with something inherent in them. What he wants to do with his holy people is, if Genesis 12:1–3 is to be believed, benefit the unholy. Readers of both the Hebrew and Christian Scriptures must hear this. *Holiness is a function not a status.* (This echoes the same point made above about being chosen, not for privilege but for responsibility.)

- The ambiguity of history.

The biblical story gets messy as it unfolds. It is shot through with ups and downs, highs and lows, sacrifice and selfishness, insight and misunderstanding. When we look at Old Testament history as an answer to the "help-we-need" we should not expect a careful blueprint. It is a messy story. Things go up and down. (And so, the upward trajectory of the *Geschichte* pattern after the Exodus, as in the various figures in the appendix, is now called in question.) What will become of the people and their mission?

Judges 13–16: Conquest

Only two individuals from the wilderness years live to enter the Promised Land—a spy, Caleb, and Moses' successor as leader, Joshua. The book of Joshua, as mentioned above, pictures the entrance of Israel into Canaan as a single, coherent, successful military campaign. Joshua, the Israelite commander, leads the campaign, battles with the other nations, divides the territory into sections for each of the twelve tribes, renews the covenant in a celebration at Shechem, and then dies.

The book of Judges, however, covers the same ground and paints a very different picture. This story is one of slow infiltration, of gradual domination here and setbacks there, of faithfulness to the covenant competing with syncretistic accommodation to the native religions—all taking place over several generations. Moreover, while this process is taking place another foreign population is attacking Canaan from the opposite direction. These people are the Philistines.

Scholars are not positive who the Philistines were, but their name, the *pilishti*, lingers down to the present day in our word "Palestine." Many have argued that they were a group of refugees fleeing from the collapse of the ancient Minoan civilization on the island of Crete. Whatever the truth may be, Judges is clear about one thing. As the Philistines push into Canaan from the coast on the west and the Israelites push into Canaan from the wilderness on the east and south—the result is conflict. The Philistines appear to have been a well-organized coalition of five city-kingdoms. The Israelites were a loose confederation of kin-based tribes with little common interest. Yet, at the end of their struggle for domination of Canaan the Israelites come out on top. How does this happen?

Judges is written in part to answer this question. Lacking a central commander, the Israelites are inspired time and again by leaders who appear, almost out of the blue, to meet various situations as they arise, and who, once the threat is past, are content to fade back into ordinary life. Each of these champions is called a *shophet*, which has been translated by the English word "judge." This term is misleading. To most English speakers it suggests an official, someone who deals with courts and criminals. While the Hebrew word can mean that too, this in no way fully embraces what a *shophet* is. Behind the notion of judging in the criminal sense is the idea of discernment, of deciding, of perceiving what is right. This is essentially what the Israelite "judges" are. They discern the times and act accordingly. The *shophet* is the one who sees what should be done and does it. The *shophet* is a heroic champion.

Our assigned chapters tell the fantastic tale of a very famous judge, Samson. The key features to note are

- the context of the struggle with the Philistines,

- the lure of religious compromise,

- the suffering on the road to success,

- and the eventual triumph that comes when the Lord is faithfully remembered.

As far as offering the "help-we-need," in comparison with the book of Joshua, the book of Judges paints a far more realistic picture of how things generally work out in real life. Judges is not only more likely as *Historie* but also more insightful as *Geschichte*—a pattern of history as help. The events portrayed are fraught with danger and vicissitudes, but they keep rolling on towards God's end. In other words, the messy, convoluted, ambiguous struggle for integrity we see in Samson rings true to the way life is for each one of us. We fight a daily battle of ups and downs in our search for wholeness. For those involved in these everyday struggles, the certain victory of Samson becomes a promise of hope. It is important to note that the object of this hope in Judges is the continuation of God's people, the bearers of the "help-we-need." Samson's fate is of little concern. At the end of his story he lies beneath the rubble of the destroyed pagan temple—but out of that rubble will come victory and new life for Israel.

1 Kings 16:21–28: Kingdom and 1 Kings 12:1–24: Split

The points to note from this reading can be made briefly:

First, Omri is a king. The period of judges ends with the establishment of Saul as the first king of Israel. In 1 Samuel the people come to Samuel, the last of the judges, and demand that they be given a king so that they can be "like other nations" (1 Sam. 8:5). In Samuel's eyes their request is in direct conflict with their calling to be holy, different, and special. After some initial hesitancy he finally agrees, and Saul is anointed king. The story of Saul's sad illness and eventual replacement by the young champion David also is recounted in 1 Samuel.[23]

David is a most successful ruler. He manages to glue, albeit temporarily, the various tribes of Israel into one nation. He creates a central capital city, Jerusalem, out of an ancient Jebusite stronghold. There he builds a palace and plans to build a temple. This latter task is subsequently undertaken by his son and heir, Solomon.

The advent of the kingship is a major departure for the Israelites. It signals an entirely new context for them. Will they be able to fulfill the promise laid on Abram so many centuries before in these new circumstances? Kings entail bureaucracies, armies, taxes, and hierarchies, all of which are in considerable tension with the nomadic people of the exodus experience. With this kingship the last vestiges of their *hapiru* past vanish away. The city replaces the wilderness as their center of identity. This tension is resolved by a restatement of the covenant, but it is couched in drastically different vocabulary. God promises that there will always be a son of David on the throne to watch over his people (2 Sam. 7). This Davidic covenant clashes starkly with the Mosaic covenant and many resist it, believing it to be a self-serving dynastic move on the king's part. Its ultimate success is due in no small part to the accomplishments of David as a ruler and later of his son, Solomon. Solomon solidifies the power of this Davidism (as I shall call it) through his building of the temple and the centralizing of religious authority in Jerusalem.

With the coming of the kingdom as a political and social reality Israel is placed, especially under Solomon, in a position to influence the nations (Abram's "all peoples") in a uniquely effective way.

But not for long. On Solomon's death his son, Rehoboam, succeeds him. Immediately Rehoboam runs into difficulties. Many see this weaker king as their chance to be free of Davidism's influence and power. A civil war threatens, the end result of which is that the kingdom is split in two.

This split of the kingdom is of huge significance. The northern kingdom takes the name Israel and the southern kingdom, loyal to Davidism and Jerusalem's cult, is known as Judah. The north is more numerous, but its political leadership is charismatic—a return almost to the context-driven leadership of the period of the *shophet.* It is subject to turmoil and uncertainty, as our verses reveal. For centuries the two kingdoms coexist in uneasy rivalry.

King Omri, by the way, was responsible for building the northern kingdom's capital city, Samaria. This city is what lends its name, for reasons we shall see, to the neighbors of the Jews of Judea and Jerusalem whom we read about in the New Testament and between whom there was such enmity. That enmity stretches back a long way, to the spilt of the kingdoms after Solomon.

The split of the kingdoms raises issues in our examination of biblical history as giving us the "help-we-need." Where is this help now to be found? Who are the legitimate heirs of the promise to Big Daddy? How can the one people of Abraham be split and still provide this help? In the struggle between God's will and the ways of the world, where are the lines to be drawn?

Problem

As an answer to the "help-we-need" Old Testament history is ambiguous. It leaves us uncertain as to how God's help will be realized for us. When things seem to go well for the people—politically, economically, and militarily—the help-we-need seems near, in the sense that God's people are in a position to influence others and yet when these same things go badly history as help eludes us again.

We still need help.

4

Torah

◆

(Exodus 20:1–17; Exodus 21:12–36; Leviticus 1, 11, 20)

Torah: A Translation Issue

"Law" is both an accurate and inadequate translation of the Hebrew word *Torah*. The root of the Hebrew word derives from the verb "to throw, shoot, point out, show," and *Torah* itself connotes instruction or teaching. (This word, Torah, is so important and untranslatable that I will no longer print it in italics. It needs to become part of our English religious vocabulary, not only in this book but generally.)

How many of us think that laws are there to teach us? We tend to believe that laws are set in place to control, govern, or protect us. We think in terms of enforcement. The seat belt law, for example, is intended to keep us safe not to instruct us on safety. There is, of course, a similarity between these two functions (enforcing and teaching) but a huge difference in nuance. Usually any legal instruction we are given (about lowered fatality rates using seat belts, for example) is designed to prompt obedience. The teaching is servant to enforcement.

Not so with Torah. Torah as law is primarily concerned with teaching. When there is an enforcement component it is intended to clarify the instruction. The enforcement is servant to the teaching.

Torah means two things: on the one hand, it is the Hebrew name for the first five books of the Bible, and on the other hand it refers to the content not only of these books but also of the entire Jewish tradition. When the word refers to the former the definite article is used and we write "the Torah." When it refers to the latter the definite article is omitted and we simply write "Torah." As answer to the "help-we-need" Torah is both.

Torah contains many rules and regulations, but this should not cloud our view of it as a whole. Its purpose is to offer guidance, aid, direction, and encouragement. The Christian image of the "way" derives directly from Torah. It is the way through life, and by following Torah we become fully human. That is Torah's promise. Above all, therefore, Torah embodies the empowerment option we have already noted. Torah is not meant to eradicate any part of us. Rather, it is meant to help us grow.

Covenant

In examining both the Flood story and Deuteronomy 7:1–9 we noted the concept of covenant. The readings for this chapter reveal its heart. At those earlier points we looked quickly at the difference between a covenant and a contract. Let us now examine that difference a little more closely.

In a contract the two parties involved share responsibility. They are equal in authority. If I contract with a company to redecorate my kitchen, for example, that company is obliged to provide its expertise and I am obliged to provide the finances. The contractor's role and my role are different, but one is not superior to the other. Failure of either party renders the contract null and void.

This is not so with a covenant. We must see the biblical covenant idea in the broader context of ancient Near Eastern warfare. Then, if an ancient king conquered a town and its surrounding area he could choose to offer the people a covenant treaty. Note that the conqueror was not obliged to make this kind of proposal. He could equally choose to slaughter or enslave those he had defeated. The offer of a covenant was *ipso facto* an act of mercy on the part of a superior (the conquering king) toward an inferior (the defeated). Moreover, the conditions of the covenant were laid out by the superior party. These conditions usually involved conduct, taxes, provision of soldiers, and the like. Generally, the conqueror, in return, would promise protection for the conquered people—as long as they undertook to do his will. The inferior party could reject the covenant offer, in which case the conqueror was freed from any obligation toward them.

Torah spells out the covenant between God and his people Israel. It embodies the covenant's content, mode of being, consequence, and promise. Christian theology has sometimes become bogged down in a debate over the relationship of law to gospel, as though one were in conflict with grace and the other not.[24] When we place Torah squarely in the context of covenant we can see that it is an expression of grace and nothing else. Torah is God trying to give us the "help-we-need." Theologians sometimes speak of the priority of the grace of God. We saw this priority in the way God treated Adam and Eve, and again in the way he treated Cain. God's attitude to his world and to humanity is grounded in his grace. Through grace God empowers us even though eradication remains a legitimate (and perhaps, dare I blasphemously say, tempting) option for him. As an expression of God's grace Torah is the supreme Hebrew archetypal story. It is the particular way Israel expresses the inexpressible.

Exodus 20:1–17: The Ten Commandments

On Mount Sinai a great event takes place. Here a new covenant relationship is created between God, the superior partner, and the people, the inferior one.[25] The superiority of God, if I can call it that, is established when he delivers Israel from bondage in Egypt. This is clearly stated in verse 2: "I am the LORD your God who brought you out of the land of Egypt, the house of bondage." God's act of power and mercy in freeing the people is the framework for the covenant. The priority of God's grace is clear, for his act of deliverance precedes the giving of the Torah.[26]

The Ten Commandments represent the heart of Torah. The various traditions within Judaism and Christianity number the commandments in different ways but all agree that verses 2 to 27 provide ten "words" (the literal translation of Exodus 20:1) of guidance. Some Jewish traditions hold that the first word is the declaration "I am the LORD your God who brought you out of the land of Egypt, the house of bondage." This numbering shows that God acted to save the people of Israel long before making any demands on them. If this statement is understood as the first word then some adjustment must be made later to still render a total of ten. This is done by counting verses three and four as one commandment. Some other Jewish mystical traditions keep verses three and four separate and maintain the right total by saying that verse seventeen (you shall not covet) is not one of the ten words but is the result of obeying them—their consequence as it were. While I very much like this last understanding, it is easier if we follow the standard Protestant numbering, not because it is necessarily correct but because it is the most familiar.

It is widely noted that the Ten Commandments fall into two halves. Commandments one to four (vv. 3–8) concern human attitudes to God and six to ten (vv. 13–17) human attitudes to one another. In some Christian catechisms these two categories are referred to as the "two tables" of the Law. What is not so obvious is where the fifth commandment, the one that involves the honoring of parents, should be placed. Many think it belongs in the first group of commandments since all parents are, in a sense, surrogates for the divine. (I suspect this view is prompted by a desire to get a neat balance of five commandments in each category.) I prefer to think that commandment five embraces both sides of the divide and serves as a bridge from one to the other. It is the hinge that holds the two tables of the law together. Let me amplify this point.

In any religion there is always a danger of thinking that faithfulness is a private and individual matter. Thus, I could approach the first four commandments and agree to use them as the chief guidance for my life. There is nothing in them that compels me to evaluate how I treat my fellow human beings. By observing only commandments one to four I could happily wallow in a private sea of piety and right attitudes to God. Commandment five forces me out of this private reverie. My parents, my family—those nearest and dearest to me, amongst whom I live, with whom I celebrate, but also with whom I often disagree—it is they who present the primary test of my faith. The fifth commandment propels me into the life of community.

Community concerns echo the deep and fundamental preoccupation of biblical faith. The very notion that God provides our purpose (that we should live in the image of God in sacred space and time) and that he also provides the "help-we-need" to do so is based in turn on his attitude, not just to me or us, but to "all people"—to the world. This is the very rationale for the incarnation principle that resounds throughout the Bible. We will hear its voice over and over—most loudly, perhaps, when we examine prophecy and when we probe Jesus' concept of encounter. In the Christian Scriptures, concern for others is heard most succinctly, perhaps, in this terse verdict: "If anyone says, 'I love God,' yet hates his brother, he is a liar. For anyone who does not love his brother, whom he has seen, cannot love God, whom he has not seen. And he has given us this command: Whoever loves God must also love his brother" (1 John 4:20–21).

Put quite simply, biblical faith necessitates community. It demands involvement with others. The incarnation principle tells us that God is with us in our lives. This, in turn, creates the incarnation imperative—that we must be there for others in their lives. Commandment five leads naturally on to commandments six to ten where community concerns are directly addressed.

Let us now briefly consider each category of the commandments in more detail.

Commandments 1–4: The Correct Human Attitude to God

What do we know of God so far? If we only count what we have learned from our present biblical reading then as yet we do not know a great deal. All we have discovered so far about God is that (a) he is the creator of life and the provider of purpose; (b) moved by his primary characteristic, mercy, he supplies us with the "help-we-need" to realize our purpose in life, and (c) that he promises to be present in power. We also know some secondary things about him, such as his power (think of the plagues) and his strange aloofness from time to time (think of how he left the people to languish in slavery for four centuries). Apart from these things we know very little. By the nature of the demands in the first four commandments however, we can conclude a few more things about him.

- Commandment One: He is to be the single object of human reverence.[27]
- Commandment Two: He is entirely distinct from creation. (see note 15.)
- Commandment Three: He is to be taken seriously.
- Commandment Four: He is to be acknowledged in worship regularly.

Thus, in addition to seeing God as our creator and helper, we can now recognize him as our ruler. Those freed from bondage (originally the people of Israel, but in some sense all who are freed from an "Egypt" that enslaves) are not to be guided and controlled by their own whims and desires. In a very real sense those free lives now belong to the liberator, the covenant maker, who sets out in no uncertain terms the attitude they are to have towards him. The traditional expressions that reflect this aspect of God are "king," "lord," and "master."

These titles seem remote and alien to our individualistic culture. Even the word "ruler" is odd. We do not naturally give a single person authority over our lives. For us, authority is institutionalized through documents (the U.S. Constitution) or ideologies (the American way of life, freedom). It is this very issue, I believe, that constitutes the heart of the contemporary crisis of belief in God. The problem is not so much God's existence as it is his *function*. People today resist being told what to do and how to live. But, this is precisely God's function as the Torah giver. And he tells us what to do and how to live, not to assert himself, but to give us the "help-we-need." Do we still believe we need help? If not then we are bound to reduce God to an ornamental or sentimental status, with no real role in determining how we should live. At best, God then becomes a nostalgic emblem, reminding us of who we once were—God as ethnic token, mere idolatry after all.

Commandments one to four stand up against this cultural trend. They demand a right attitude to God that, in turn, results in a new view of ourselves. *If God is ruler, it must be that we need to be ruled.* Being ruled is a form of the "help-we-need." And if we need to be ruled, it must be because a self-centered attitude to life is wrong.

"I" must be involved with "you."

Commandments 6–10: The Correct Human Attitude to One Another

The first use of the word "sin" in the Bible, as we noted, is in the context of the Cain and Abel story. It is human violence that brings about the Flood in the Noah story. In the archetypal framework of the Bible wrong relationships are the major cause of disruption. By placing the commandments on right relationships after those that concern the correct attitude to God, Torah acknowledges that community must be rooted in faith. If "God is dead" we can do whatever we want, and doing whatever we want means that someone is going to get hurt. Aggressive self-assertion always ends in violence. Equally, however, Torah insists that faith entails community, as the proclamation of commandment five establishes. Right relationships express a right attitude to God. A faithful community both resists violence and is the absence of violence.

There is a common principle running through each of the five commandments of the second table. We are not to murder, be faithless with, steal from, lie about, or covet the possessions of our fellow human beings. In short, we are to respect them—to treat them as we would be treated by them. This is the opposite of aggressive self-assertion, which is sin. The Golden Rule finds its nourishment here: Jesus and other rabbis (not to mention the Buddha, Confucius, and even Kant) each in their own way said, "Do unto others as you would have them do unto you." And this is the heart of the Ten Commandments.

To sum up—the Ten Commandments teach us to respect who God is, who we are, and who our fellow human beings are. This respect amounts to taking God and what he cares about seriously. There are three parties in this equation: God, self, and the other. Thus when Jesus was asked what he thought the meaning of Torah was he answered, "You shall love the Lord your God with all your heart, and with all your soul, and with all your mind.... You shall love your neighbor as yourself" (Matt. 22:37–39.)[28]

Exodus 21: Everyday Details

How very different in tone these verses are from the lofty Ten Commandments passage. What are we to make of the ideas in this passage—about diminishing a wife's food, about knocking out the tooth of a servant, about an ox goring a man or falling into a pit? What has all this got to do with faith in God?

Everything. It has everything to do with faith in God because this faith must spill out into our relationships with others. This spilling out involves *every aspect* of our interactions with them. Too easily we are tempted to think that we meet the requirements of religious community building if we are nice to each other about narrowly religious matters, if we smile and greet one another at church or synagogue—while all the time we backstab and manipulate in the market place. These verses show us how broad the love of neighbor must be. It must extend over every aspect of our lives. It must reach into the kitchen, the byway, the office, and the farmyard. All are sites for the expression of holiness, no less than the sanctuary.

Torah is all embracing.

Scholars sometimes speak of two categories of law in the Hebrew Scriptures: apodictic law and casuistic law. Apodictic means "incontrovertible," carrying the implication that such law is spoken from God in an absolute sense and without qualification. For example, "thou shalt not kill" is apodictic law. Casuistic law, on the other hand, is case-based and takes the form of "If...then..." While both types express the will of God, casuistic law derives from community living while apodictic law expresses the nature of God himself. Apodictic law is indelible and permanent, while casuistic law is open to qualification and modification.

It is worth noting that this issue about the unchangeability of law came to occupy a great deal of attention in the Christian Scriptures during the formation of the early church. Christianity was coming to see itself as an entity distinct from Judaism—distinct from but, as it turned out, not all that different. Very soon after it had rid itself of much of Torah's casuistic law, the church busied itself in the formation of its own body of minute rules and regulations, collectively known as canon law.

However illuminating this apodictic-casuistic distinction may be, it should not be allowed to intrude into the reality of Torah. Torah has both, expresses both, and needs both. There are not two Torahs, one apodictic and one casuistic, one more true than the other, one more essential than the other. The lofty commands concerning one God, no idolatry, no murder, and so on, are not on some different plane from the issues of how to manage a crazy bull in the field. Each expresses Torah, guidance for living the life that God wants. As such, each embodies the "help-we-need."

Leviticus 1, 11, 18: More Details

Each of these chapters illumines the breadth of Torah's concern and embrace.

Chapter 1: Sacrifice (For more on sacrifice see the next chapter in this book, Ritual.)

Most members of religious institutions are familiar with the notion of giving an "offering." This normally means making a financial contribution for the ongoing work of that institution. Sometimes (although rarely) these contributions are sacrificial. They are the result of prayerful thought, budget concerns, or sometimes just lazy carelessness. Offerings are often referred to as "free-will offerings," thus emphasizing the individual's desire to determine how much to give and what to give it to.

The first chapter of Leviticus is entirely different in tone. Very little is left to the free will of the worshippers. What happens to their offerings—how, when, and why—is clearly defined. Torah covers even the smallest details of religious practice.

Chapter 11: Clean and Unclean

The beginning of this chapter, verses 1 to 23, introduces the idea that some foods are permitted while others are not. We all have subconscious notions and taboos about food. How many of us would relish eating horse, or rat, or snake? Some people do eat these meats, but most of us would rather not. In other words, we have some innate sense of permissible and forbidden foods, even if this sense is highly individualistic. In common with the entire thrust of Torah, this area is not left up to the individual. The Ruler will rule here too. Some animals are *tahor*, clean, and others are *tamei*, unclean. (*Tref*, a word commonly used by modern Jews for unclean, derives from Yiddish not Hebrew.)

The second section, verses 24 to 47, broadens the concept of clean and unclean. In the Hebrew Scriptures the concept comes to be applied to many things other than animals and food—including, for example, buildings (a house with fungus), natural aspects of life (a menstrual woman), and many other particulars of normal life. We must realize that in using the vocabulary of clean and unclean we are not talking about physical hygiene but of ritualistic and religious acceptability. It is sometimes argued that some of the dietary bans, such as the eating of pork, are based on hygiene—that it would have been hard to preserve pork in the climate of the ancient Near East. But, why would pork be singled out as unhygienic? Left unrefrigerated lamb goes bad, too. Hygiene as a basis for the *tahor* and *tamei* categories collapses entirely when it is applied more broadly. Why would the mixing of dairy products with meat be a problem? Is beef stroganoff unhygienic? And why would *tahor* and *tamei* apply to non-food issues as well? The entire matter of clean and unclean must be traced back to theology, not hygiene. It is a reflection of the creation dynamic of separation that we saw in Genesis 1. God seeks, through Torah's clean-unclean dynamic, to remind his people of his ever-present concern with all aspects of their lives.

Chapter 18: Sex

It used to be that the Rotary Club, in extending an invitation to a guest speaker, would politely point out that any subject was acceptable except "religion and politics." What else interesting is there left to talk about? Why, sex, of course.

While I do not think this is what the Rotary Club had in mind, the Bible anyway will not avoid confronting the issue of sexual relations. Chapter eighteen in Leviticus covers the subject in great detail. I do not intend to go through these verses one by one, but once again it is important to note the breadth of Torah. Torah belongs in the field, the shop, the temple, the kitchen, the highway—and the bedroom. Torah belongs everywhere because everywhere we go we need help.

Problem

Torah seeks to give us the "help-we-need" by providing guidance and direction in life—for all of life—so that we might "be holy" and thus realize our purpose. The problem is that the help it offers depends on our response, and we inevitably fall short.

We still need help.

(See Figure 14 in the appendix for an illustration of this dynamic. Each Voice we shall be examining is also illustrated in the appendix.)

5

Ritual

❖

(Exodus 35:4–29 and 36:8–38; Leviticus 23;
1 Kings 6; Nehemiah 8)

Sacrifice

In our last section, in looking at Leviticus, we briefly mentioned sacrifice as an example of the scope of Torah. Let's now examine it more deeply.

It is difficult for modern readers of the Bible to come to terms with the idea of ritual sacrifice. We must try, however, to understand the intention behind it.

Often ancient civilizations believed that their gods or goddesses needed to be fed and ritual sacrifice fulfilled this obligation. We can see this, for example, in Greek mythology in the story of Persephone and Demeter, in which Hades abducts Persephone and carries her off to the underworld. Her mother Demeter, the goddess of grain, goes into deep mourning. Her mourning and grief continue unabated, and the earth falls fallow. This becomes a concern to Zeus and the other gods because without crops the humans cannot make their sacrifices. The story continues, but what we learn from this much of it is that, in some sense, the mighty Olympians need what human sacrificial worship provides. Zeus and his heavenly colleagues are in some sense sustained by the earthly sacrifices.

Many religions in the ancient Near East, in Europe, as well as in the Americas, structured kingship around sacrifice. In some cultures at a festival marking the beginning of the New Year a young man would be selected as consort to the heavenly queen. He would reign for a year, after which he would be put to death. Other cultures offered their first-born to the gods as a token of all that was most precious. In the Hebrew Scriptures we hear echoes of this through the regulations provided for redeeming the first-born.[29]

There are indications in the Old Testament that child sacrifice was a practice encountered in that ancient environment. The lure of the world, the desire to "be like other nations," might well have prompted the people of Israel to imitate this horrible activity. Many scholars maintain that animal sacrifice evolved as a substitute for child sacrifice. This is illustrated literally in Genesis 22 where the haunting and challenging story of the binding of Isaac is related. Just at the moment when Abraham takes his knife to slay his son he is interrupted and given a more acceptable sacrifice—the ram with its horns caught in the thicket nearby.

Whatever the historical origins of sacrifice might be, by the time the Hebrew Scriptures had settled into their final form the practice of offering grain and fruit and of sacrificing animals had become an expression of faithfulness. They were the heart of Israel's religious ritual. What are we to make of this?

The letting of blood, the taking of life, was a symbol and recognition of the perilous nature of the transition from life to non-being. This transition, which we refer to as "dying," was made perilous because of human sinfulness. Sinfulness constituted a threat to the successful life—that is to say a life pleasing to God. It was believed, however, that sacrifice could nullify the effects of sinfulness. For example, inadequate expressions of thanks could be compensated for through sacrifices. Repentance could be expressed the same way. Sacrifice was not a mere token of an attitude but the incarnate representation of it. The goods to be given up were costly and total. Were the worshippers willing to offer or slaughter what was precious, even most precious, to them? By carrying through with the sacrifice, they could transcend falsehood and pretence. They also could verify the authenticity of their faith and the integrity of their character. Again, the story that best illustrates this in the Hebrew Scriptures is Genesis 22—the sacrifice of Isaac—mentioned above. (This incident is so important that Muslims also tell it, using as the victim Ishmael, the legendary father of the Arabs.)

Sacrifice was a literal intersection of death, life, guilt, and forgiveness. When sacrificial blood was spilled all that would make the transition from life to any being beyond life either impossible or problematic was removed. This is captured in the famous text from Isaiah 1:18, "Be your sins like crimson, they can turn snow-white; be they red as dyed wool, they can become like fleece." The worshippers' lives, red with sin, became symbolically white through the spilling of the red blood of the sacrificial animal.

Accordingly, sacrifice was a most serious activity. Not surprisingly, the details of the ritual were carefully prescribed and punctiliously observed. We can see this faithfully reflected in the readings for this section.

Exodus 35:4–29 and 36:8–38: Certain Place

Note the extraordinary level of detail in Exodus 35:4–19. God, in commissioning the tabernacle, stipulates an entire color and fabric scheme. It is almost as if he had a divine passion for interior design. Nothing is left to chance. Even the minutiae of the furnishing and utensils are regulated. This passionate concern for particulars is "what the LORD has commanded" (Exodus. 35:4). Here we see God as the detail-oriented one. His will is to be seen and found even in the smallest of things. All together his plan for the tabernacle expresses something of his message, of the help he seeks to give us. (This, by the way, is a fundamental of good religious architecture: design bears meaning; structure is symbolic; the details proclaim. Many contemporary religious buildings are driven by merely practical concerns—acoustic requirements, location impact, and the like. These are important considerations, but all too often they swamp symbolism. We are left with sanctuary as cinema.)

A good example of the power of symbolic meaning is the color scheme God requires for the tabernacle. It comprises blue, purple, and scarlet. Purple, of course, is what we get if we mix blue and scarlet together. In the ancient world blue symbolized the sky, while red (scarlet) symbolized the earth. (Remember the meaning of the name "Adam" in Genesis?) Purple is midway between the two, embracing the hues of heaven and earth alike. The tabernacle is where sky/heaven/God and earth/the world/humanity meet in ritual. The colors are a simple promise, expressive of *ehyeh asher ehyeh*: "I (the blue) am *here*, in this sanctuary (the purple), as the one who will be *there*, out in the world of your every day life (the red)."

The first key point about ritual as an answer to the "help-we-need" is that it offers a *certain place* to encounter God.

Throughout all the upheavals of life, amidst all the arenas where we can wander and become lost, ritual is always there as certainty. Here, God says, I will be present for you. It is not that God cannot be anywhere and everywhere else. Indeed, one of the Hebrew titles for God is *Ha-makom*, "the place,"—meaning that any place we happen to be is also and simultaneously a place where God is. As we noted, this was the meaning of Torah's all-embracing scope; wherever we are is a place for Torah faithfulness. Nevertheless, some locations can seem distant from the "everlasting arms." (See Deuteronomy 33:27. Some translations offer an alternative phrase, but the new Jewish Publication Society uses this one. I retain it, not only because it is possibly accurate but also because of its beauty.) Not so where ritual occurs, for there God promises he will be. His presence is certain. Every place may be a place of encounter, but equally may not be. This "perhaps" quality is removed in ritual. The tabernacle/Temple is a *certain place* for encounter.[30]

Leviticus 23: Certain Time

The fourth commandment tells us that the Sabbath day is to be kept holy. Exodus 20:8 traces the institution of this holy day to the seventh day of Creation during which God rested. *Shabat* in Hebrew means "to rest." The Sabbath ordinance encourages us to mimic the rhythm of God's creating process in our weekly lives. It is a form of *imitatio dei*.

(Interestingly, in the form of the Ten Commandments found in Deuteronomy 5:6–21 the reason given for the Sabbath is different. Here the Sabbath day is to be remembered because God delivered the people from slavery and he, presumably unlike Pharaoh, wants to give them the occasional day off. Possibly this difference in rationale derives from the fact that in Exodus 20 the Ten Commandments are attributed to God directly whereas in Deuteronomy 5 they are attributed to Moses. Thus, God himself gives a cosmic reason for the Sabbath, while Moses gives a historical reason.)

As the Sabbath is to the week so the special days we read about in Leviticus 23 are to the year. Like the details in the tabernacle design these days are to be arranged with great precision. Their dates are laid down by God. In Genesis 1:14 we read, "Let there be lights in the expanse of the sky to separate day from night; they shall serve as signs for the set times—the days and the years." The Jewish religious calendar is to be calculated by lunar-solar interrelationships. (Christians, frustrated by the interruption of school vacations by Easter, sometimes plead for a "fixed Easter." By this they mean an Easter that would fall on the same day every year—the first Sunday of April, say. What they fail to grasp is that Easter, like these Hebrew festivals, is already fixed by the sun and the moon, however inconvenient this may be.)

As with the Torah, so too is it with ritual. In each we discover the detailed nature of the will of God. It is easy for us to imagine God concerned with grand designs and broad sweeps, but in Torah and ritual we hear and see him involved in the minutiae as well. Little things count for him, and they should count for us too if we want to receive the help on offer.

Here is the second key point about ritual as an answer to the "help-we-need": it offers a *certain time* to encounter God.

Time runs away from us. The future becomes the past before stopping long enough in the present to become familiar ("future shock" as it has been called[31]).

As one scholar says, time is a "familiar stranger."[32] But, this is not so with ritual. Ritual brings time to a stop in the sense that ritual is a certain time, a time when God has promised to be with us. Because the time for ritual is so precisely mapped out, worship is rescued from human feelings. It is not that we are to worship or pray when "we feel the need," but rather when God has prescribed. Surely one of the most powerful images in our modern world is that of Muslims, including in their number some of the world's wealthiest and most powerful people, answering the five-times-daily summons to prayer. Muslims may pray when they feel like it, but they will also pray at the set times. Such obedient regular prayer, called *salat*, is one of the so-called five pillars of Islam.[33] Structuring time according to the expressed will of God makes a temple out of all time as it passes, an embodied mimicking of the ways of God. Time is not a meaningless flow to extinction. It has meaning. Church observance of the Christian year reflects this belief.

1 Kings 6: The Temple

There are two important points that emerge from this chapter.

- *The certain becomes the necessary.*

Amidst all the incredible detail, echoing as it does what we have already noted in reference to the tabernacle, verses 11 to 13 stand out. Here they are:

> Then the word of the LORD came to Solomon, "With regard to this House you are building—if you follow My laws and observe My rules and faithfully keep My commandments, I will fulfill for you the promise that I gave to your father David: I will abide among the children of Israel, and I will never forsake My people Israel."

These are very revealing words. Ritual has been elevated to awesome significance in the life of ancient Israel. Faithful ritual now guarantees that God will be God. But something strange has happened. Unpack the logic in these verses:

1. *If* the Ritual is done according to God's will, *then* God will be with Israel and never leave them.

2. *If* Ritual is faithful, *then* God will be amongst his people.

3. *If* the sanctuary is sacred, *then* all places will be.

When we come to examine power in our next section we will have more to say about how ritual is forced into serving the Davidic covenant system and scheme (what I have called Davidism). For now, it is enough to note that the freely given tabernacle presence of God amongst his people, through the construction of the temple and the correct performance of worship in it, suddenly seems to have been rendered conditional, however unintentional this may be. The promise of the presence of God anywhere and everywhere the tabernacle was transported has now become dependent upon his certain presence in the constructed Temple on a specific site and therefore at a place chosen by humanity. God's radical presence has been given an address. Ritual is hereby elevated to a place beyond all other modes of *ehyeh asher ehyeh's* being with his people. While ritual is the guaranteed presence of God, other places and other times are shot through with wild conditionality. Indeed, to be in the *certain* presence of God a person is now *required* to be *in the temple at the right time.*

Are seeds of despair being sown? What will happen to faith if the temple—the place and time of God's certain presence—is destroyed, if the performance of the ritual is no longer possible? If nationalism is a policy of protecting national institutions, including the temple, does this view of ritual verge on making nationalism a necessity? And if this is so, will the nation come before God? Where are we if we are somewhere far distant from the certainty that ritual offers? Will we be nowhere—a place of no real significance? *Ha-makom* is "no place." Who am I *then*? Will I still matter to God?

• *The necessary becomes the only.*

Solomon's temple, as described in this chapter, comprises two areas: the Holy Place and the Most Holy Place (the Holy of Holies.) This reflects the structure of the wilderness tabernacle, although the temple is many times larger. The Most Holy Place can be entered only by the High Priest and then, as prescribed in the regulations, only on the Day of Atonement. A vestibule is added to the Holy Place and the Most Holy Place. In 2 Chronicles 4, two "courts" or courtyards are also mentioned. These are the court of the priests and the great or large court for the laity.

The building plan, therefore, creates the sense of an increasing intensity of God's presence. Later, the social ideology of decreasing access is added so that fewer and fewer people can get close to where God's power is most concentrated. Later, the larger court for the laity would be divided into two areas, one for women and children, and the other for adult males. Beyond these courts would be an area where anyone could move about, Jew or Gentile. (See Figure 21 in the appendix.)

This notion of increasing holiness accompanied by decreasing access is seen in medieval Christian cathedrals, in which large screens were built across the nave, cutting off the choir from the area for the laity. The choir, in turn, was then divided by screens or steps from the chancel area where the high altar was located. It was here that the sacrifice of the body and blood of Christ took place. Only a priest could approach. In such cathedral churches God was literally cut off from his people, and they were denied direct access to him. (Today's penchant for churches that look more like cinemas than cathedrals has, alas, deprived us of an appropriate sense of awe. We are left searching for God's presence in the preacher's words or in the music of a praise song. Amplified sound overpowers mystery. Nobody would be spontaneously tempted to remove their shoes in such churches—that overpowering sense of standing on "hallowed ground" has been lost.)

Problem

Ritual seeks to give us the "help-we-need" by offering us a certain sacred space and time to be with God. Here we receive the encouragement needed to realize our purpose—which is to live everywhere and always in sacred space and time. Yet we saw that a problem can easily arise when the place of guaranteed sacred space and time becomes *the necessary and thus the only* such place.

We still need help.

6

Power

◆

(1 Samuel 8–11 and 15–18:16; 2 Samuel 5; 6; 7:1–17; 11–12:25; 24; 15 and 18–19:18; 1 Kings 4:20–6:38; 9:15–28; 11:1–13; 2 Kings 25)

A Flawed Failure: King Saul (1 Samuel 8–11 and 15–18:16)

Like Other Nations

As we saw earlier in the history section the people come to Samuel, the last of the judges, and press him to anoint a king for them. Their explicit desire is to be "like other nations." Samuel resists this request because of his theological conviction that God alone is the people's king. Also, he probably sees there is tension between the people's desire to be like other nations and their special responsibility to God. After all, the entire point of the call and promise to Abram was that his descendents were to save all nations from the common human predicaments of Genesis 1 to 11. They were not supposed to join them and become like them.

The story of the selection of Saul reads almost as if God finally gives in and says: "Oh well, alright. If they insist, then go ahead." There is very little enthusiasm for the idea. The best Samuel can say of Saul, apart from the fact that he is the man of God's reluctant choosing, is that he has quite a physique. 1 Samuel 8: 23–24 tells us that Saul is the tallest man in the land, and it is because of this that Samuel decides to commend him to the people. It is not a very convincing reason. We should take note, too, of Saul's attitude. He tries to avoid being acknowledged as king as if he too shares Samuel's doubts. Indeed, the atmosphere of hesitancy in these passages clearly points to a *Geschichte* perspective. This not a neutral recital of "what actually happened."

Uncertain though Saul may have been, his first action as king is a resounding success. He summons men from all the tribes of Israel, forms an army, and then leads it out to crush a threat from a foreign power, worried by this new king situation in Israel. His triumph is referred to as the "Lord accomplishing salvation."

His next military venture, however, leads to problems. All warfare is brutal but ancient warfare was particularly so. One common tactic of that time that specially offends our modern sensibilities is the *cherem*, or "the ban." All the captured living things of a defeated enemy were slaughtered—men, women, children, and animals. There was a rationale behind this. The ban eliminated the possibility of future threat, it removed the possibility of retaliation, and it offered a ritual sacrifice to the divine power that had made victory possible. In his battle with the Amalekites Saul implements the ban, to "kill alike men and women, infants and sucklings, oxen and sheep, camels and asses" (1 Sam. 15:3). The *cherem* order is clear, unambiguous, and not very unusual in the context of those days. But Saul spares the Amalekites' king, Agag, and he also spares the best of the livestock. The result of Saul's disobedience is instant, total, and irrevocable. Immediately, we read, God rejects him as king and Samuel is sent, in 1 Samuel 16, to anoint a new king.

Saul, the first king of Israel, is a disaster. His reign, however, does not lead to a renunciation of the concept of kingship. On the contrary, his throne must be filled by a more suitable candidate.

Transition

1 Samuel 16 tells the story of the selection of David. Samuel arrives at the home of Jesse who introduces seven of his sons to him. Samuel's verdict is that not one of them has been chosen by God. In response to Samuel's enquiry, Jesse admits that the youngest son is away tending sheep, the clear implication being that he was never considered as a royal possibility. He is fetched and, of course, God informs Samuel that this is the one. David is anointed king of Israel then and there. Israel has two kings simultaneously.

Immediately we begin to read of Saul's increasing depression, of his need to be soothed. The only way to comfort Saul, to mend his troubled mind (to provide therapy) is to surround him with beautiful music. (Down to this day this is still a therapeutic technique.) A young musician is brought to him, and it turns out to be none other than David. David is taken into Saul's service, and we are told that he becomes his ever-present servant and armor-bearer.

David and Goliath.

1 Samuel 17 reads very differently. The famous story of David and Goliath seems to know nothing of the tradition of David as musician/armor-bearer. We

have evidence here, as we did with the Noah's Ark story, of the redactor interweaving at least two traditions. The concern in this rendition is with the transition of kingship from Saul to David. The Bible, we must ever remember, is a redaction throughout. The redactors did not strive for some neutral, never-happened harmony, but rather they purposely placed parallel stories side by side to highlight the individual truths and insights contained within them.

Clearly the 1 Samuel 17 story has a different source from 1 Samuel 16. David is not strumming his harp to soothe the commander king. No, in this story Saul is facing the Philistine army and its huge champion Goliath—enough to disturb any general—while David is back home watching over the family flocks.

We read that David arrives in the Israelite camp to visit his brothers. He is amazed to learn that nobody is ready to challenge the daily taunts of Goliath, and without hesitation he volunteers himself. News of this reaches the king, and he and David duly meet.

Perhaps the most revealing detail in the David and Goliath story is found in 1 Samuel 17:38–39. One thing the two traditions have in common is their interest in Saul's armor. In this story Saul offers it to David for his pending battle with Goliath. I will return in a moment to the symbolism of this, but for now let us consider how this would have worked. Saul, as we noted above, was the tallest man in Israel. Sunday school illustrations have often depicted David as a little boy during this incident. Why, if David was just a little boy, would Saul have offered his armor? Indeed, the story goes on to say that David attempts to put it on. And this is the armor of the tallest man in the land? It makes no sense whatsoever. For Saul's offer to be remotely plausible David must have been nearly as tall as Saul. The reason he rejects it is not because of its size but because he is not used to it. He boasts to Saul about his shepherd's ability to kill wild beasts with his bare hands. David is no little boy. We must see the contrast between David and Goliath, not so much in terms of size, but in terms of experience. Goliath the Philistine relies on his professionalism. David, a tall but raw young man, relies on the guidance of the Lord in whose name fights.

The immediate (and unlikely if David were a mere boy) consequence of Goliath's defeat is a huge enhancement of David's reputation and a diminishment of Saul's. David's popularity soars as Saul's crashes. Symbolically, David has indeed put on Saul's armor, the trappings of kingship. The references to Saul's armor in the two traditions are a symbolic way of indicating David's slow usurpation of Saul's popularity and position.

Scholars have written extensively about the double tradition of the transition from Saul's kingship to that of David. Our purposes are served, not simply by noting the double tradition but also by understanding the interplay between God's will and human ambition—Saul's, David's and the peoples'. Each tradition is shot through with the unrelenting progress of David's rise, impelled either by popular will (the people clearly idolized him) or by his own ruthless, but superbly controlled, aspirations.

Power, or rather the use of power, is rising as a motif.

A Flawed Success: King David (2 Samuel 5; 6; 7:1–17; 11–12:25; 24; 15 and 18–19:18)

Jerusalem
Salem was an old Jebusite city and a well-situated stronghold. From the start David understood the military importance of this fortress, and as soon as he was king of Israel he launched a successful campaign to take it over. Once it was conquered he changed its name from Salem to Jerusalem, and he made it into his own impenetrable power base. From here he was able push the Philistines back to their coastal areas and effectively put to an end Israel's long struggle with them. David then took the huge step of having the sacred Ark of the Covenant brought up to Jerusalem.

The Ark was in essence a box, carried on poles. The people had been commanded by God to construct it at the time of the creation of the Tabernacle. It was a holy symbol, perhaps ancient Israel's most holy symbol. The armies would have it carried before them into battle, ensuring, they believed, God's presence with them and thus also ensuring ensuing victory. In this box Israel's most sacred objects had been placed—tradition says, the tablets containing the Ten Commandments, manna from the wilderness days, and Aaron's magic rod. It served as a tangible indicator of God's presence amongst his people and was Israel's holiest object. By bringing it up to Jerusalem David was removing it from the random control of this or that tribe. By establishing it under his own protection he asserted his kingly authority in a highly symbolic way. Jerusalem was not only the capital city of a nation but also uniquely the center of David's power under God.

It is also worth noting that David seems to have made some kind of deal with the incumbent religious authorities of Salem. Genesis 14:17–20 tells the story of a priest of that city, Melchizedek, coming out to greet and bless Abraham with a ritual of bread and wine. Melchizedek represented the Jebusite priesthood. These priests were called Zadokites—the word being related, some believe, to the New Testament "Sadducees." David allowed these Zadokites to remain in place in Jerusalem as guardians of the Ark. In undertaking the primary priestly duties they effectively displaced the Levites, the sons of Aaron. From this time forward the role of the Levites was reduced to that of ministers of music—the choir.

David's taking of Jerusalem was a supreme power move.

Covenant

1 Samuel 7 describes this power more explicitly. We noted earlier how the use of the ancient wilderness notion of Covenant slowly became applied to David personally—embodying the promise that his heirs would be kings forever. This was the creation of what I call Davidism. There is a tradition, related to the therapist/musician strand, connecting David to many of the psalms in the Bible. Whether he personally penned any of them is a moot point, but it cannot be denied that many of the psalms celebrate kingship and elevate it to a position of centrality in Israel's self-understanding. These particular psalms are now regarded as coronation hymns. They might well have been sung at festivals reenacting the enthronement of the king. Others are placed in the context of the ups and downs of a king's reign, describing external enemies and internal tensions. In them the king asks for, and expects to get, the help and support of God in his troubles. Such royal psalms were a major propaganda tool of Davidism. This Davidism would remain in tension with other more ancient modes of self-understanding.

The rise of kingly power caused problems.

Bathsheba

The Bible never makes allowances. The story of David and Bathsheba is a story of adultery, murder, the death of the innocent, and the birth of a son. Underlying it all, however, is the reality of the use and abuse of power.

Nathan the prophet, in his parable of the rich man, quietly and effectively skewers David on the sharpness of his own flawed character. David's shortcomings are writ large for him and for all who read of him. The Bathsheba incident reveals the root problem with power.

As we saw in the stories of Cain in Genesis 3 and the tower builders in Genesis 11, sin is the assertion of power, of self over the rights of others. In the Bathsheba incident David puts his needs, his desires, and his preferences over any and all other considerations. That is why his prayer for the baby born of the adultery goes unrequited. He must come to realize that he cannot master matters of life and death. (Later a son would be born to David and Bathsheba—and that son would be Solomon.)

Absalom

David's youth and abilities had attracted people away from Saul. Later the youth and abilities of David's eldest son Absalom did the same to him. Both manipulated and manipulator Absalom was not unlike his father. Absalom attempts a coup against his father and seems on the brink of success. David is forced to flee Jerusalem, leaving his capital city to the rebels. The setback is only temporary, however, and in the struggle that ensues Absalom is killed. David's grief, so eloquently expressed in its brevity, is the hollow heart of power's residue. Absalom's willful assertion of self in the end brings only pain and suffering to his father—and death to himself and many of his followers.

David

David is a fascinating man. The Bible's portrait of him is richly compelling in its honest recognition of his flaws and its glowing praise of his virtues. In the end, however, we have to acknowledge that David is a supreme example of power. He never fails to seize the day, the opportunity, and the chance. He seeks to take control, to be in charge, and to shape history. He never hesitates to use tradition to serve his vision of Israel's role in the world. But is his vision God's vision? David ushers in the advent of power on the biblical scene. How will it play out?

A Flawed Future: King Solomon (1 Kings 4:20–6:38; 9:15–28; 11:1–13)

Success and Temple

Solomon is successful on a wider stage than his father. Due to power vacuums in both Mesopotamia and Egypt, Solomon is able to establish Israel as a major player on the stage of ancient world affairs. Under Solomon Israel finds itself in a strong position to influence "all nations." 1 Kings 4:20ff sums it up: Judah and Israel were as numerous as the sands of the sea; they ate and drank and were content. Solomon's rule extended over all the kingdoms from the Euphrates to the land of the Philistines and the boundary of Egypt. They brought Solomon tribute and were subject to him all his life. God endowed Solomon with wisdom and discernment in great measure, with understanding as vast as the sands on the seashore.

Everything seems to be in place. The phrase about the sand on the seashore echoes God's promise to Abraham concerning his descendents (Genesis 22:17). What would Solomon do with this wonderful opportunity?

Solomon builds a temple. This does not strike us as being in conflict with the Abrahamic promise and mission. His father David had been denied the privilege of erecting the temple, but to Solomon it was a logical sequel to bringing the Ark of the Covenant to Jerusalem. We saw in our last chapter on ritual how the temple slowly became an exclusive place of worship, edging out all others. This had a huge effect on the theological self-understanding of the people. But in simply building the temple, Solomon could not have foreseen these results. Instead, to him the future must have appeared bright, certain, and full of promise.

Discordant Notes

The verses that summarize Solomon's other achievements use the same words that governments everywhere use—taxes, conscription, orders—all implying increasing control over the people. Power can quickly lead to privilege and privilege to the abuse of power. Bound by the conventions of the time, Solomon enters into political treaties and alliances that entail him marrying foreign princesses. They, in turn, demand that their own religions come along too. Solomon caves in. Temples to foreign Gods begin to appear in Jerusalem.

Power has asserted itself and the self has moved into a place of central value. Solomon has decided to allow his policies, preferences, and the pressures he was under in a practical sense, to control and determine his decisions, rather than mere faithfulness to the covenant Lord. This is the assertion of self. This cannot go on.

God intervenes. His verdict is that Solomon has broken the covenant and forgotten the ways of the traditional faith (1 Kings 11:11.) This faith refers only to the Mosaic covenant—and not to the kingly covenant of Davidism. Indeed, these verses can be read as a condemnation of Davidism and its arrogant belief that it could supplant the covenant of Sinai. God condemns Solomon and predicts disaster. Civil War is just over the horizon.

Flaws Realized: Decline, Fall, and Exile (2 Kings 25)

And then disaster—one we looked at briefly in the history section. In about 900 BCE civil war threatens and nine of the twelve tribes desert Davidism. They abandon Jerusalem—its ideology, palace, and temple. Only Judah, Benjamin (by force), and the Levites are left in the south to express the Davidic covenant's form of hope.

The period of the two kingdoms (Israel in the north and Judah in the south) will be looked at again in the chapter on prophecy. Suffice it for now to observe that, despite efforts at reform, this is a period of social, economic, and religious decay and decline.

In 721 BCE the Assyrians, on their way to do battle with Egypt, invade the northern kingdom of Israel. Ashurbanipal's army all but obliterates Israel from the map. With the exception of a small remnant left in and around their capital city Samaria, nine of the twelve tribes of Abraham's people vanish from history. Eighty-three percent of the people of God who were to bring the "help-we-need" to the world vanish.

But the disaster is still not played out. The Babylonians, having solidified their power in southern Mesopotamia, conquer Assyria and begin to turn their eyes towards Egypt. Judah is right in the way. In 587 BCE the Babylonians enter the southern kingdom and conquer Jerusalem itself. Scholars debate about what happened next—whether, in fact, the Babylonians took most of the population to Babylon or merely the leaders and the intellectual elite. Whatever the exile entailed, its impact was brutal. Gone were all remnants of Davidism. This ideal had proven impotent before the Babylonian gods and generals. From this time on, and for many centuries to come (indeed until the Muslim conquest in the eighth century CE), Babylon would be the intellectual center of Jewish life.

A return to Jerusalem does indeed take place, as we shall see, but Jerusalem never recaptures its role as the intellectual center of Israel until the post-Shoa period. (The Shoa—literally "whirlwind"—is the Hebrew name for the Nazi holocaust.)

Problem

Power seeks to give us the "help-we-need"

- by removing history's ambiguous kind of hope and taking control of it through the king;
- by embracing Torah's scope and focusing the incarnate power of God in the king;
- and by expanding ritual's arena and dignifying politics through the king's personal covenantal relationship with God.

The problem with this is that pouring all the resources for the "help-we-need" into power submits and conditions this help to the harsh demands and vagaries of secular limits. Suddenly "God," as the source of life and the provider of help, is no longer needed. Power as embodied in the king is the ultimate assertion of self, the very sin of Genesis 11: 1–9.

We still need help.

7

Wisdom

◆

(Jeremiah 18:18; Proverbs 1; 9; 12;
Ecclesiastes 1–3; Job 1–2)

Jeremiah 18:18

This little text throws a lot of light on religious life and practice in ancient Israel.

We are going to learn a great deal more about Jeremiah in our next section. For now we should simply note that he is one of the great prophets of Israel. We see him at work in Jerusalem in the late fifth and early sixth centuries BCE, a little over one hundred years after the northern kingdom has fallen to the Assyrians. Now, the new threat to the nation's life is Babylon, a threat Jeremiah clearly sees and one those in power dismiss as insignificant. Jeremiah's repeated warnings against smug self-confidence turn the leadership against him. Jeremiah is the classic illustration of the "prophet of doom and gloom." A prophet with a difficult message is never popular. Jeremiah is arrested and his life is under threat. More of him soon.

Based on Jeremiah 18:18 we can conclude some things about the groups that conspire against Jeremiah. Part of their concern is to preserve the religious establishment. They see Jeremiah, not Babylon, as the threat. We can see this point of view summarized in our verse. Here three functionaries are identified, each with a religious role. The priest is the expert in giving law (*torah*), the prophet in proclaiming the word (*dabar*), and the wise man in offering counsel (*etsa*). All three groups oppose Jeremiah in an effort to preserve their place in the religious hierarchy. Each, in some sense, is a supporter of Davidism. They look to that hope to save them, while Jeremiah simply dismisses it as any kind of guarantee.

We have already encountered the figure of the priest. The priest is essential to the temple ritual and the sacrificial structure. Without him the service of worship can not proceed. As for the prophet, we will discuss him further in the next section.

But what about the "wise man?" To what does this refer?

Scholars have devoted a great deal of energy in recent decades to the study of Hebrew wisdom. Wisdom literature is a highly distinctive area of religious expression with its own specialized style of writing. Many have noted wisdom traditions in other ancient Near Eastern religions, especially that of Egypt. The wisdom tradition was hugely influential throughout the period of the creation and redaction of the Hebrew Scriptures.

Of all the Bible voices we have examined so far wisdom will probably be the least familiar to most readers. This is a pity. The wisdom tradition played a major role in ancient Israel and may well have had a considerable influence on the Christian Scriptures as well. In our little text (Jer. 18:18) the wise man is placed on a par with both the priest and the prophet.

The wise man (*chakam*) is filled with wisdom (*chokmah.*) This Hebrew wisdom, however, is not wisdom as an idle academic pursuit. The Hebrew wise man is not given to solitary contemplation or individual enlightenment. Greek *sophia* is the concept that lies behind the western philosophical tradition (*philia* "love" plus *sophia* "wisdom" together make our word "philosophy" meaning the "love of wisdom.") The western philosophical structure is neatly packaged under headings that embrace wide-ranging fundamental questions. For example, the study of epistemology asks: What is knowledge? The study of metaphysics: What is real? Ethics: What is the good? And the study of logic: What is valid? Hebrew wisdom is very different from this. *Chokmah* cannot be so easily analyzed and categorized. Its concern lies elsewhere.

The purpose of Hebrew wisdom is understood only as it is expressed as *etsa*—counsel. Essentially this *etsa* is wisdom as it is applied to life. In short, Hebrew wisdom is highly practical. Its mission is to help its students steer a right course through life. Further, the wise man is a teacher by definition. Hebrew wisdom is not to be hoarded but shared. It is about life, for life, and in life. Some scholars believe the Hebrew wise man's students were limited to future members of the royal court—think, a professor at the Kennedy School of Government. Others believe wisdom was taught to any and all who wished to learn. Our purposes (to hear wisdom as an answering voice to the "help-we-need") can be served without entering this debate.

While bits and pieces of this wisdom are found throughout the Hebrew Scriptures (for example in the famous story of Solomon and the two arguing mothers in 1 Kings 3:16–29) three biblical works stand out as wisdom literature *par excel-*

lence of the Hebrew Scriptures. These are Proverbs, Ecclesiastes, and Job. In examining selections from each of these books we will be able to identify differing emphases within the Hebrew wisdom tradition. We also will see how rich and multi-faceted they are as tools for life's journey.

Despite their differences, however, these three books have one thing in common, and it is a thing of particular interest. This one thing is their silence on certain subjects. We will read wisdom's pages in vain for a point of view on the great march of *Geschichte*, the detailed instructions of Torah, the sacrificial promise of ritual, or the secular ambitions of power. It has nothing to say about the voice of prophecy. Wisdom is a self-contained vision. It speaks as a lone voice to Israel, isolated from Israel's other voices. Wisdom teachers seem to have turned their backs on any dialogue with these other witnesses.

Does this silence inform? Does it suggest that wisdom and wisdom alone has a claim on vision and that the other voices should be ignored or at best tolerated? In turn, what vision of God do the wisdom teachers have in mind? Is he a self-revealing God in any sense?

As we proceed, these questions can be in the back of our minds.

Proverbs 1; 9; 12: The Wisdom of Cause and Effect or Commonsense Wisdom

Proverbs 1: Introductory Summary.

Throughout Proverbs Solomon and other kings are mentioned as being in some sense responsible for the contents of the book. The traditional view is that Solomon actually composed all or many of the proverbs. This may be so—but it may also be that the proverbs simply were taught in one of the training schools for the kings' advisors. Or, on the other hand, they may just have circulated during the time of the monarchy. Certainly the book was gathered from different periods of time, and a variety of hands lie behind its composition.

Chapter 1 serves as an introduction to the collection. As such it introduces some of the fundamental categories that characterize the rest of the book.

Pragmatism

The opening verses indicate that somehow what follows is intended to help steer the student of wisdom through life. The teaching is, above all, applicable. *Chokmah* is neither speculative nor theoretical. Its guiding principle is usefulness.

Methodology

A rich recipe of verbal forms is introduced, amongst which are riddles, sayings, parables, and proverbs. Some scholars have devoted considerable energy to the study of these various forms and their linguistic nuances, seeking to identify differing roles and contexts for each.[34] We should simply note that wisdom is a supremely verbal phenomenon. Just as wisdom in general is driven by pragmatism, so too is its language driven by the need for clarity. Wisdom is, as we could say, user-friendly. This is hard to detect when reading it in English since its entire word-play dimension is lost in translation.

Education

The devotion to linguistic intelligibility reveals another central premise behind the wisdom tradition. It assumes that people are able to grasp and incorporate guidance for their lives. Wisdom is transmitted through education. We can almost sense a classroom setting. Wisdom teachers do not preach or pontificate (the second not necessarily the same as the first) but they explain, cajole, correct, and encourage. They are instructors above all else, and the phrase "instruction-for-life" might well be used as a synonym for wisdom.

Types

Our chapter, Proverbs 1, introduces three main kinds of people. Each of them will be described in greater detail in the remaining chapters of Proverbs. These three types exemplify a way of understanding life. The issue is to determine which one will come to dominate.

On the one hand there is the wise man or teacher. This teacher is in some sense always a student. (I am reminded of the time I heard the great C. H. Dodd, perhaps the most renowned English New Testament scholar of the twentieth century, describing himself to a gathering of glittering biblical academics as "a student of the New Testament.") In Proverbs the voice of the teacher is often portrayed as Lady Wisdom, a personification of Wisdom itself.

On the other hand there is the fool. In wisdom literature folly is not simple ignorance. By "folly" the wisdom teachers means, first, ignorance that is a choice and, second, any behavior that is based on that ignorance. Folly often appears as Woman Folly.

In between these two is the young man or pupil. A polarity is set up between wisdom and folly. They are the two guides, and the student is the locus for their contesting voices. As he listens to both he must learn to discern between the two. Will his choices reflect his training in wisdom or his natural attraction to folly?

God

Proverbs 1:7 states that the "fear" of God is the beginning of "knowledge." This verse is echoed in Proverbs 9:10 where it says that such fear is the beginning of "wisdom." Two points need to be made. First, fear in this context does not mean terror. It means awe. In recent times the word "awesome" has become trivialized. At the same time, awe—a sense of being in the presence of the ineffable—seems to have disappeared from our routine worship experience. Because of this, the notion of the fear of God is alien to many of us. Properly speaking, awe is the way we feel when we are in the presence of something utterly different from and hugely more powerful than ourselves. It is accompanied, paradoxically, by a strange sense of lure and comfort.[35] This is the kind of "fear" that is the foundation of wisdom. Second, we must understand God here in terms of Proverbs itself. This is where the note of silence, the musical rest, comes into play. In wisdom's God-talk Israel's other experiences are barely acknowledged. We can glean very little about the wisdom teachers' theology. It may well be, of course, that they simply assumed a broader experience, but the silence about this should caution us. We will have to look more deeply into Proverbs to discover how the wisdom teachers understood God and their relationship to him.

Proverbs 8 and 9: Life's Fundamental Charter and Choice

Here we see the wisdom student, our young man, caught between two contending, feminine voices—Lady Wisdom and Woman Folly. We might well wonder why wisdom—which the biblical wise men follow, seek to teach, and to which they are devoted—is personified as a female. Is this a compensatory reaction to the massive patriarchalism of ancient Israelite society and its male-dominated vision of God? Is it an echo of the ancient religious environment in which Israel was formed? The religion of the native Canaanites for example, was Baalism. The word "Baal" means lord and he was often pictured as a bull, frequently with consort goddess figures. Because Baal was a strong male image he required some kind of female balance. Perhaps this same thought process is at work in Proverbs. Certainly, in the chapters we are looking at Lady Wisdom claims a pre-existent status and even a role in the process of Creation itself. Indeed, her claim for authority in this life (vv. 32ff.) is based precisely on this semi-divine status. Her joyful pre-existent intimacy with God is a guarantee that allegiance to her teaching will bring abundant life. This leads directly to a graphic contrast in Proverbs 9 between Lady Wisdom—modest and comely, whose ways lead to a controlled existence and eternal rewards—with Woman Folly—loud and lewd, whose enticements lead only to entrapment and death. Lady Wisdom offers a banquet of life whereas Woman Folly's guests "are in the depth of the grave" (Prov. 9:18). Which voice will capture the student's attention and heart—and soul?

Proverbs 12: Commonsense Miscellany

The breadth and scope of the wisdom in this chapter is secular and humanistic. The proverbs here could easily have leapt off the pages of Benjamin Franklin's *Little Richard's Almanac*. Without the all-encompassing "fear of the LORD" concept introduced in Proverbs 1 we would be hard-pressed to identify these verses as religious in nature at all. That, however, might tell us something about our view of religion. For here these proverbs are—in Scripture and as part of the Word of God—articulating an answer to the "help-we-need." What then do they say to the basic human cry for help? Two important aspects must be noted. The first is wisdom's focus on the individual, and the second is its elevation of commonsense pragmatism.

It is not the worshipping community, nor the Torah-loyal people, but the individual who is summoned to respond in these wisdom proverbs. It is up to the student to choose between Lady Wisdom's dinner party and Woman Folly's sleepover. This decision is desperately real. The young man is totally free to choose, but the consequences are enormous. The individual mind and heart is where these options intersect. Wisdom teaching is like basic military training. It is a tough course and one that will prepare the individual for the struggles ahead. Further, success or failure will have lasting future implications in terms of life and death. The fact that this book is addressed to an individual is new in the Hebrew Scriptures—and for it to do so effectively it requires a new voice.

More, a fundamental cause-and-effect dynamic is at work in wisdom. Choose this way and all will be well. Choose the alternative and things will go very badly indeed. Pragmatism is elevated to the level of all-encompassing truth. If something works it is wise. If it does not work it is not only foolish but useless. One wonders what the wisdom teachers would have to say if challenged, for example, about ritual as the "help-we-need," or about such laws as *tahor* and *tamei*, the clean and unclean distinction. Would they dismiss these things as useless or unworkable in the life of the individual? Would wisdom teachers dismiss institutional religion? Do we hear wisdom teachers all around us today?

To sum up, we can conclude that in Proverbs wisdom is cause-and-effect commonsense aimed at the individual.

Ecclesiastes 1–3: Courageous Despair at the Limits of Wisdom

Like Proverbs, the book of Ecclesiastes has sometime been attributed to Solomon. However, its author is now regarded by most scholars as an unknown "preacher" or *koheleth* in Hebrew (Ecclesiastes 1:12). Koheleth's work can be regarded as a counter-voice to the up-beat commonsense of Proverbs. Proverb's pragmatism suggests not only that the student has the choice but that, if he makes the right choice, all will be well. Koheleth will have none of this naiveté.

Two themes dominate Ecclesiastes—work and wisdom. Over and over again Koheleth asks what "profit" there is to either. The equivalent expression today would be: What's the point? Koheleth's answer is given in 1:2 and 12:8: "Utter futility!—said Koheleth—Utter futility! All is futile!" The Hebrew word that has variously been translated as "futile," "vanity," or "meaningless" is *havel,* the root of which is "mist." Work, wisdom—life itself.—is as insubstantial as mist. All is hollow. As Ecclesiastes 1:7 so eloquently puts it, nothing ever feels filled. Emptiness is the chief characteristic of life.

Religious faith doesn't help, according to Koheleth, for God makes the sun rise equally on the righteous and the wicked. Prosperity comes to both, regardless. So what then is the difference between wisdom and folly? Nothing, he concludes in 2:15. It is as if Koheleth is arguing that since God shows no discernment, why should we?

What then is the best course? Hedonism? Koheleth tries self-indulgence and it, too, produces only the same feelings of hollowness and meaninglessness. A life of instant pleasure and gratification is *havel,* after all.

Koheleth means it when he says "all" is vanity. His vision is radical and inclusive. Nothing escapes his verdict. For him there is nothing in life but mist.

The famous passage on time and times in 3:1–8 offers little comfort. Read in the context of Koheleth's attitude it suggests a general resignation to circumstance. Time for dancing? Great. Time for weeping? So be it. This is the opposite of Proverbs' aggressively optimistic tone, where the student is summoned to design his own destiny by his own good choices. In Ecclesiastes the individual must passively take whatever arrives in its "time."

Yet, the wise man's face shines (8:1). When death comes, as it must, he has some modest satisfaction, even though it is hard to verbalize his advantage over the fool. His wisdom consists in knowing that he cannot know (8:16–17).

If for Proverbs wisdom is a kind of pragmatic omni-competence, for Ecclesiastes it is a courageous despair. Koheleth not only recognizes the pointlessness of it all, but he also bravely accepts things as they are. In writing it all down, even though "there is no end to the making of books" (Eccl. 12:12) Koheleth will not go silent into the night. He wants to be heard—and our hearing it is wisdom.

Job 1–2: Moral Outrage as Wisdom's Vision

Briefly put, Job will not despair. Job will not bend, nor break, nor give in. Job is outraged at the unfairness of life, and he grounds this outrage in the highest level of morality—the very nature of God.

We should read the entire book of Job to catch the full blast of its message. The little folktale of chapters 1 and 2 is used merely to set the stage. Modern readers may balk at the notion of God playing with Job in order to win a bet with the Satan, but as a fairy tale it works as well as any other fairy tale, dealing in an almost whimsical way with the serious issue of good and evil. Satan's argument with God is based on his view that Job's righteousness is not the real truth about him, that his prosperity and good fortune fuel his faithfulness. Take the outer circumstances away, Satan wagers, and the true character of the man will be revealed.

This is the setting for the magnificent dialogues that follow between Job and his comforters. The essence of his comforters' advice is based on the wisdom ideology of Proverbs—that of pragmatic cause-and-effect commonsense. According to this, Job is suffering because he deserves to. He has committed some sin that has precipitated all the evil that has come to him. Job must have slipped off into the house of Woman Folly. Proverbs teaches that the individual is the center of responsibility. Thus, Jobs' friends argue that the individual is equally the center of reward and punishment. Job's suffering is punishment for his wrongdoing. In order to ameliorate his situation he must repent.

It is against this ideology that Job rails. He asserts his innocence over and over. His friends cannot accept his assertion. To do so would be to destroy the whole edifice of their wisdom. In essence, the book of Job argues that wisdom breaks down in the face of innocent suffering. The common sense of Proverbs breaks apart on the harsh realities of actual life. Moreover, and at the same time, Job rejects Koheleth's courageous despair. Job will not despair. He is outraged. Job has been a wise man and a good student. He cannot bring himself to jettison these traditions of wisdom because of his circumstances. He wants answers. His suffering is fuel for his outrage and as the book unfolds, his impatience mounts until it busts forth.

"For I know *that* my redeemer liveth, and *that* he shall stand at the latter *day* upon the earth." (Job 19:25, as the Authorized Version translates it.)

Many are familiar with this text. They have heard it sung countless times in Handel's Messiah, always in a peaceful, soft, and reassuring voice. It is a beautiful aria—but, from a biblical perspective, it is actually a terrible cry of anguish. With it, Job plays his last card. He demands a fight with God. He is willing to take on God Almighty, but only if there is a neutral referee, "my redeemer."

There are many psalms in the Bible that scholars refer to as "Songs of Lament." They are complaints. Few if any of them approach the passion of Job's complaint. In the face of his suffering and the meaninglessness wreck his life has become he takes issue with God himself. In this far frontier of human experience wisdom in the book of Job encourages rebellion against the Life-giver in the name of life itself. Proverbs' common sense *quid pro quo* wisdom has collapsed; Koheleth's courageous despair is too shallow and self-centered. Job wants more. He demands answers.

Job's cry amounts to a clarion call for help. His is the voice of moral outrage. We need help. Job demands it.

Problem

Wisdom, paying little if any attention to Torah, Ritual, and Power, seeks to speak in a very unique voice. It gives us the "help-we-need" by trying to make sense of life as it is (Proverbs); by bringing morality into the realm of the bearable (Ecclesiastes); and even when it runs into its own limits, by raging against the light to make protest a virtue (Job). All of these, each in its own way, seek to make the notion of usefulness or applicability the central criterion. Each gives its own *etsa*. The problem with this is that by limiting the "help-we-need" to the category of the useful, God is removed to the realm of the merely inscrutable.

We still need help.

8

Prophecy

✦

(1 Kings 17–19; 21; Isaiah 6; 5:1–7; 9:1–6; 10:22–11:16; Jeremiah 2–3; 13:15–27; Ezekiel 37:1–14; Haggai; Zechariah 1:1–6; 2–3)

The Clash

(See the appendix *Idiot Sentences Four and Five* with their corresponding diagrams, Figures 9 and 10.)

It is crucially important to note that the next voice, prophecy, arises in the midst of the established kingdom.

In essence, prophecy is a collision of faith's uncompromising promises and demands with the compromising realties of a life controlled by power, characterized by ritual, and resigned to the voice of wisdom. It reasserts the unpredictable covenant-making reality of the God of the desert times. Once again we hear the Word of God in the famous prophetic phrase, "Thus says the LORD." The prophetic voice refuses to use God to foster the assertion of self above all else (as power does), to remove God to the realm of the inscrutable (as wisdom does), or to lock God up in an exclusive place of sacred space and time (as ritual does.) The prophetic voice reinforces the life-embracing demands of faithful obedience (as Torah does.) It is true that Moses, a pre-kingdom figure for sure, is referred to as a "prophet" (Deut. 34:10–12), but this clearly is a tradition articulated in the years after the ministry of those we now refer to as "the prophets." The prophets who concern us just now are the great canonical spokesmen of God whose ministry was directed over against all other established religious authorities—kings, priests, wise men, and the other so-called "prophets."

When reviewing the Cain and Abel story we detected a note which resounded in the story of the Tower—namely, the tension between differing views of the ideal life. Urban life in these stories is portrayed as less than ideal. Over against this is the elevation of Jerusalem as the ideal place, as the site of the temple—where, in the Holy of Holies, the very presence of God is made real. In some ways it could be said that the royal ideology, Davidism, is simply an example of the incarnation principle being restricted to king and city.

The prophets come into this context with a very different word. It is a word of confrontation. This confrontational dimension of prophecy must never be overlooked. We noted tension in the people's desire for a king in the first place. This tension was made especially clear in Samuel's overt reluctance to give in to their wishes. Now this hesitancy comes back in full force in the freewheeling, bold, unleashed voice of prophecy.

The Hebrew word for a prophet is a *nabi*. The root of this word gives the sense of one in whom the spirit "bubbles up and bubbles over." Thus, the *nabi* is bursting with a word. He cannot stop speaking it. He must let it out. The English word "prophet" comes from the Greek *pro* meaning "for, on behalf of" and *fero* meaning "to carry." A prophet carries something on behalf of someone else. The prophets we will look at, and the others they represent, carry God's word or message on God's behalf.

When Moses received his call at the burning bush, he was reluctant and hesitant, even to the point of arguing with God. He was convinced that God had made a mistake. We see this over and over again in the calls of the prophets. Each is characterized by unlikelihood. They are either too young (Isaiah), too rural (Amos), too tied down (Hosea), or too unqualified. (Can anything good come out of Nazareth?) That, however, is the very point to glean. With prophecy the messengers and their qualifications and characteristics are not the point. The point is wholly the message of the sender. What counts is the prophecy not the prophet. If you have ears, then hear.[36]

In essence, prophecy speaks the unlikely word—either of doom and judgment to the self-satisfied and proud or of hope and courage to the despairing and defeated.

Elijah and Elisha: 1 Kings 17-19; 21

The drought, the contest on Mt. Carmel, and the issue of Naboth's vineyard are emblematic of the confrontational context of prophecy. The king and his wife, together with their religious establishment, are castigated and eventually conquered by the agency of the message-sender, God. Elijah (and later Elisha) is an agent of judgment. His message is one of doom and destruction in the face of wild complacency and abuse. The exception, of course, is the incident of the widow's son, raised to life in the midst of rampaging death. The widow and her son are exceptional because they aid and encourage the messenger. The prophets—in desperate straits and making no pretence at asserting self—are anti-types of the power exemplified by the king and queen. They surrender their wills and their lives to God and in their submission receive life.

Notice, though, that even with a vicious ruler such as Ahab a word of repentance can stay the doom. As we have seen from the story of the Garden on, God's mercy triumphs. True, Ahab will eventually plunge to destruction, but not until his spiritual stance changes once again. So long as he remains repentant, so long is God merciful.

The key to understanding prophecy and the relationship of the messenger to the message-sender is found in the incident of the cave.

Elijah has fled for his life. He is feeling sorry for himself and, believing he alone is the sole remaining champion of God, he takes refuge in retreat. He holes up in a cave. In this setting, of secluded, safe, personal protection, God asks Elijah the probing, challenging question: "Why are you here?"

Elijah's explains his outward circumstances. He fails, as we so often do, to catch where the emphasis in God's question lies. Elijah hears: "*Why* are you here?" He answers accordingly and, with patient detail, recounts his faithful exploits under the most difficult of circumstances.

God repeats the exact same question. Surely the tone and accent is unmistakable. "Why are you *here*?" God wants him to be out in the world of confrontation no matter how difficult it may be. Has he forgotten *ehyeh asher ehyeh*? Why is he *here*, in a cave, isolated from the world to which he has been sent? God so loves the world, remember?

Elijah's failure is not one of political courage but of theological discernment. Now, lest it escape our notice, God gives Elijah orders to anoint kings in countries where there are already kings in place. Elijah, who has run from the world to keep himself safe, is to wreak political havoc, to cause revolutions, to overturn governments. It is no coincidence that the cave story ends with the introduction of his successor, Elisha. God is done with Elijah. God sees what we can so easily forget—that to protect self at the expense of faithful witness is a form of self-assertion. It is biblical sin.

Isaiah: Isaiah 6; 5:1-7; 9:1-6; 10:22-11:16

Isaiah 6 is a chapter frequently read at the ordination and installation services of new pastors. This is because it is believed, rightly, that presenting oneself for ordination is a response to a call, a response to God's question, "Whom shall I send? Who will go for us?" Isaiah's answer is deemed appropriate for all such pastors: "Here I am; send me." If we examine the passage more closely we will note that some caution is called for. (A text without a context is a pretext.)

In this chapter Isaiah recounts how he was called to be a prophet in about the year 742 BCE. Upon the death of King Uzziah Isaiah wandered into the temple. It is important to keep in mind that huge hopes had centered on Uzziah. He seemed to be wise and dedicated, with an authentic desire to reform the religious-political establishment. (The story can be read in 2 Kings 15.) In itself this observation is important. Now he had died. The first ingredient in the context of Isaiah 6 is of hopes dashed. Naturally, the king's death had caused anxiety amongst the reformers. Had the promise of change died with him? Note especially: reform was needed. Society had become corrupt and the religious establishment with it.

All of this is the context for the call of Isaiah, which took place that day he wandered into the temple. In effect, God was saying: you, Isaiah, are now to continue the work. The king, Uzziah, is dead. Long live the prophet, Isaiah. As we have noted with Moses he protests his lack of qualifications. He is unclean. He is unworthy. God touches his lips. This ritual declares the reformer pure enough to carry out the task of reform. No more excuses.

This also explains the oddly pessimistic first pronouncement of the new prophet in verses 9–12. The people will not listen and disaster will arise anyhow. But, at least a tiny remnant (v. 13) will survive. Hardly the stuff of an encouraging ordination sermon.

Isaiah, however, is soon busy with his new work. In chapter 5 he brashly and boldly announces that God's "anger" (v. 25) is "roused" and is ready to be unleashed against Israel. The opening parable of the vineyard makes clear the cause. Israel, God's chosen people (Gen. 12), have turned their backs on their calling and have indulged in social, political, and economic injustice and immoral selfishness. As a result, soon, very soon, a mammoth reversal of fortune is going to occur, with suffering for the cruel and exile for all.

Yet, interspersed with these threats of wild and all-encompassing devastation there is a word of hope. Chapters 9 and 10 speak of a new king, another start, a return to peace, justice, and equity. Amidst the darkness a small light flickers.

Jeremiah: Jeremiah 2-3; 13:15-27

In chapters 2 and 3 of Jeremiah, we hear loud protests against the social injustices already made familiar in Isaiah. (See especially the chilling summary in 2:34 "On your garments is found the lifeblood of the innocent poor.") In addition, there resounds a note of horrified disapproval of an old crime, embraced with new enthusiasm—idolatry.

Israel is accused of changing its God for "no-Gods," of switching its allegiance from the rescuing and powerful Lord of Exodus to that which "can do no good" (2:11). The fount of living waters has been forsaken in favor of leaking cisterns. Nobody is innocent. All have participated—especially those who ought to have known better, who should have led the fight against such tendencies—Israel's kings, leaders, and priests (2:26).

Jeremiah prophesied in the southern kingdom of Judah. Decades earlier the northern kingdom of Israel had been overrun by Assyria and Jeremiah understood full well the impact of this devastating loss. He knew how tenuous the strand was that connected the people of Abraham's promise to their God. He sensed that strand was about break.

Later Jeremiah summarizes his message. "Woe to you Jerusalem, who will not be clean. How much longer shall it be?" (Jeremiah 6:8.) Something terrible and dark is about to happen. Jeremiah sees the gathering armies of Babylon, looming military defeat, and the exile of his people.

He sees the end of Davidism.

Ezekiel 37: 1-14

Not all prophets speak a word of doom and gloom. The coming darkness prophesied by Isaiah and Jeremiah (also by Amos, Micah, and others) arrived, of course, and in 587 BCE Israel was led into exile in Babylon.

The profundity of this disaster is hard to exaggerate. Scholars are uncertain who actually was taken into exile. Some argue that only a limited number of people were involved—mainly Judah's political, religious, and intellectual leadership. Others believe the number was far greater and involved almost the entire population.

The point to keep in mind, however, is that the significance of the Exile was not quantitative, but qualitative. It was an event not unlike the sacrifice of Isaac in Genesis 22. The real issue then for Abraham, in being asked to sacrifice Isaac, was not just the loss of his beloved only son but also of God's promise for the world's salvation, bound up as it was with the boy's life and future. So it was with the Exile. All seemed lost—Jerusalem, temple, palace, Davidism—all the tradition of faith that saw God as great and good. The God of the Abrahamic promise either had made a huge mistake or had disappeared altogether. After all their long, suffering history, the people of Israel were more or less right back where Abraham had begun some 1500 years earlier. Surely God, the God of Abraham, Moses, and David, was weak, if real at all. Surely, the gods of Babylon were mightier. It was all so deeply sad. It was no wonder the people wept by the waters of Babylon (Ps. 137) as they recalled what once had been.

Into this exilic context of despair and doubt, Ezekiel speaks a profound word of hope. He prophesies to a valley of dry bones. The people and their faith were skeletal—dusty, immobile remnants of what they had been and what God intended them to be. Yet here, into the abyss Ezekiel flings the word of resurrection (37:12–14). He talks of the power that will bring the people back to where they belong, where they long to be. Israel will rise again. Exile will give way to new life. This is empowerment such as we have never encountered in the Bible before. This is resurrecting power. It carries the reality of *ehyeh asher ehyeh* beyond hope, beyond this life, to realms of new possibility otherwise inconceivable.

Haggai and Zechariah: Haggai; Zechariah 1:1-6; 2-3

Each of these prophets refers to Darius. Darius was the name of a Persian king.

Empires rise only to fall. Babylon had successfully dealt once and for all with their northern Mesopotamian neighbors, the Assyrians, and had dominated the ancient empire of Egypt. The empire was long thought to be impenetrable, but then it entered a period of decay and decline under its new king Nabonidus. The Babylonians became a dispirited and exhausted force. In the end they fell with astonishing ease. Cyrus, who had managed to combine the eastern powers of Media and Persia, conquered Babylon in 539 BCE, and this once great power disappeared from the stage of world history.

In the city Cyrus discovered a group of foreigners, Jews, who spoke to him of their crushed capital city, Jerusalem, and described how the Babylonians had looted their temple. Cyrus issued a decree allowing the people to return home, along with their temple treasures. It is very little wonder that the Old Testament hails Cyrus as the *mashiach*, the messiah, the anointed one, the Christ (Is. 45:1). The people were free to go. The dry bones had flesh on them once more, just as Ezekiel had promised.

We must understand the situation. Babylon was, by ancient standards, a huge and cosmopolitan city. Jerusalem was a backwater town. Why go back? What was waiting there? Ruination and rebuilding. Most of the exiles were reluctant to return. The Exile had lasted a mere sixty years or so, but it was long enough that most of the Jews in Babylon had been born there. Babylon was home. (As we have already noted, Babylon would remain the intellectual center of Judaism for centuries, up until the Muslim conquest many centuries later. When Jews refer to "the Talmud" they almost invariably are speaking of what is known as the *Babli*, the Babylonian Talmud, testifying to Babylon as the center of authority and vitality of Judaism despite the later return from exile.) Born and bred in New York City, as it were, it is hardly surprising that many did not want to return to Podunk.

Yet, Cyrus persisted. He appointed a governor and provided the means for the people to return. Now it was understood what an earlier prophet of the Exile (called by scholars Deutero-Isaiah—a disciple of the Isaiah we have already met) had been speaking of when he said, "A voice rings out: 'Clear in the desert a road for the LORD. Level in the wilderness a highway for our God. Let every valley be raised, every hill and mount made low'" (Is. 40:3–4). This prophecy was to become fact. Across the desert to Jerusalem the people were to retrace the steps of salvation first taken by Abraham over a millennium earlier.

Not everyone returned—but some did. What they found was not the glorious city and temple their grandfathers had told them of with such longing. All was ruined, decayed, plundered, overgrown, and gone. They quickly realized that the main issue of the day was survival, scraping a living out of the land and re-establishing some sort of agricultural infrastructure. Their least concern was rebuilding a religious edifice.

Into this context come Haggai and Zechariah. Scolding, cajoling, promising, pleading, they manage to get the people to gather enough energy to rebuild the temple, not on the scale or with the grandeur of Solomon's building, but at least a temple faithful to the requirements of ritual as answer to the "help-we-need."[37]

Is it not amazing? The voice of prophecy, birthed in collision with power and what power had made of Israel, closes in service to ritual.

The period of second-temple Judaism had begun.

Problem

Prophecy seeks a response, variously using threat and promise. It speaks the word from God into a life of satisfaction and despair, seeking to stimulate a life of justice and hope. The problem is that its success as answer to the "help-we-need" is as fragile as our response.

We still need help.

9

Apocalyptic

❖

(Daniel)

Stabilization

In order for us to have a chance at understanding the apparently weird and fantastic genre of apocalyptic, we must first know something of the more normal aspects of Israel's life in which this genre arose and flourished.

At the close of our examination of prophecy I introduced the phrase "second-temple Judaism." Let me unpack the reality of this a bit more.

The experience of exile and restoration had an enormous impact on the way the Jews thought about themselves and their life with God. In many ways the Exile was a time of enormous creativity and, indeed, it can be argued that in and through the Exile Judaism, as distinct from the ancient Israelite religion, came into being.

Most scholars place the redacting process of the Pentateuch and the beginning of the collecting of the Prophets in this time period. In addition, (as mentioned under the "Ritual" heading) cut off from the temple, the people had to find a new way of worshipping. Out of this need grew the institution of the synagogue. (Interestingly "synagogue" is a Greek-based word, deriving from *syn* meaning "together/with" and *agein* meaning "to lead/drive/herd." It corresponds exactly with the Latin-based word "congregation," deriving from *cum* and *gregare*.) At synagogue worship, in place of sacrifice by priests, there would be prayer and praise, and the people would listen. The Torah was read, often having been rendered into Aramaic, a Semitic language closely related to Hebrew and then spoken by the people. (These Aramaic readings were later collected and known as *Targums*.) Additionally, at the synagogue worship someone qualified would explain and apply the reading. This is the origin of the sermon.

Jewish thought traces its rabbinic ministry back to this foundation. The collective name "the men of the Great Synagogue" was applied to the "preachers" of this time and, moreover, tradition went on to claim that the explanations and applications given by them were in fact part of an oral tradition extending back to Moses on Sinai. (One scholar speaks of this as the dual Torah tradition.[38]) Something of this is reflected in the story of Ezra recounted in Nehemiah 7:73–8:18.

In other words, as the people came out of Exile they came with new religious institutions, Scripture and synagogue; and new religious authorities, the precursors of the rabbis. They also emerged with a new sense of their own fragility as God's people before the nations. The recent experiences of exile and restoration had become guiding lights for their self-understanding. Rather than far distant events in the past these were now the norms for current self-understanding.[39] Life was newly understood as uncertain and unstable. Their own history of infidelity and the presence of powerful foreign enemies were fresh ingredients in their faith expression. What they urgently required was a sense of stability.

To a great extent the rebuilding passion of Haggai, Zechariah, and others (see Ezra 3–6) was really a program of stabilization. So, too, were the ministries and missions of Ezra and Nehemiah. (Notice that Ezra and Nehemiah are the final two figures of *Idiot Sentence Five* in the appendix.) The correct chronology of these two figures is unclear. Who came first? Scholars are divided. The broad outline, however, is sure.

With Persian permission, Nehemiah was sent to Jerusalem to rebuild its protective wall. Ancient cities were walled—encircled by a reinforced barrier with gates to permit passage in and out. These gates could be shut tight against enemies. As long as Jerusalem's wall lay in ruins there was no stability for its inhabitants or those in the neighborhood who could flee to it for protection when they were threatened.

Ezra arrived in Jerusalem to build another kind of wall—a wall of racial and ideological purity. Many returned exiles had intermarried with the people who had infiltrated the land—land Ezra regarded as Jewish soil. He saw this alien presence as a threat to Jewish identity.[40] Ezra called for mass divorce of foreign wives and a repentant return to the ways of God. All this is recounted in Ezra 9 and 10.

In short, in post-exilic, second-temple Judaism, the overriding desire was stability.

As it happened, the ancient world was about to be stood on its head. Everything was about to change—in an instant. Stability would soon be an impossible dream.

The Europeans

(Refer to Figure 2 and *Idiot Sentence Six* in the appendix.)

In 336 BCE a king in far-away Greece died and was succeeded by his young son, Alexander. The Persian Empire, already weakened by revolution in Egypt and internal corruption at home, was poised to fall. (The rise and fall of nations is one unmistakable incidental lesson to be learned from reading the Bible as a whole. Is this a secret reason why we avoid reading it and remain satisfied with favorite and familiar snippets? Is this a lesson from history that we do not want to learn?)

Alexander was more than a military genius and conqueror. Tutored by none other than Aristotle he had been taught that Greek culture (its language, philosophy, theater, sports, education, and religion) was the pinnacle of human achievement. He set out, not simply to conquer the world, but to colonize it. This process is now referred to as hellenization. Alexander's armies swept out of Europe and, at the battle of Issus in 333 BCE, he routed Darius III, the Persian king. With this victory, the way into Asia lay open. In swift order, Alexander took Egypt, Mesopotamia, and Persia. By 323 he had reached the Indus River. Everywhere he went Greek culture was imposed on the populations. Whole cities of the ancient world turned Greek almost overnight. Jerusalem was no exception.

In the face of hellenization's enormous pressure on all peoples to dress as Greeks, speak Greek, and even to worship Greek gods and goddesses where could the foundering Jewish nation find stability?

Daniel

The book of Daniel is made up of two very different sections. Chapters 1 to 6 are the story of a Jewish hero, Daniel, and his friends who, in the face of anti-Jewish legislation in exilic Babylon, remain faithful and are ultimately triumphant. Chapters 7 to 12 are very different. They describe four strange visions: one of four weird beasts; the second of a ram and a goat; the third of seventy weeks; and the fourth of an angel and the future.

Many scholars believe that chapters 1 to 6, while set in Babylon and speaking of its king, Nebuchadnezzar, actually reflect the situation of Jews in Jerusalem under the Greeks in the early and middle second century BCE. Chapters 7 to 12 also speak of the Greeks, with specific reference to one of their most cruel and zealous rulers, Antiochus, who gave himself the title "Epiphanes" which (like the Christian festival Epiphany) means "manifestation." He thought he was the manifestation of the gods. The Jews gave him the nickname, *epimanes*, which means "crazy." He instituted policies of such severity against all things Jewish and enforced them with such cruelty that they bordered on the insane. One reaction to the Antiochene policies was to fight. (We will look at the Maccabean revolt later.) Another reaction was to dream of a new world order, of a time when fortunes would be reversed, the oppressor gone, and the people free. Daniel's visions offered such dreams.

To have such visions is dangerous both for the dreamer and for those with whom the dreams are shared. How can the oppressor be referred to so he will not recognize himself? How to predict his imminent downfall without detection? How to communicate hope for a new day?

The writers of apocalyptic created visionary poetry, with allusions in code to contemporary events and figures. The code was known to those on the inside, the intended audience, but remained hidden and obscure to anyone else. Hence apocalyptic, as in such books as Daniel, speaks of strange monsters, odd images, weird events, and supernatural agents.

The urgent question for apocalyptic is not who or how—but when. For the writers of apocalyptic time was of the essence. The passion to know just when all political and social misery would be blotted out is clearly seen at the end of Daniel 12. Seeking to reassure his readers, the author says that resolution, what he calls "the end of the days" (12:13), would come about in a year, plus two years, plus half a year (12:7)—that is in 1277 days. But, sadly the end did not come as predicted. In Daniel 12:11 it is recast as 1290 days, and then in the next verse this is extended to 1335 days. Verses 14 closes with the simple advice—keep on till the end.

While apocalyptic so clearly promises stability in time to come, a promise very familiar to biblical tradition, it includes a dimension deeply at odds with the Abrahamic vision. The apocalyptic end, whenever it comes, will result in the destruction of "them" and the preservation of "us." Indeed, "they" are the servants of all that is anti-God and, because of this, deserve obliteration. Gone from apocalyptic is any sense of God's love for the world—a love so thorough that "we" are to be used to save "them." (We shall hear more of this voice in the next section.)

Apocalyptic is the voice of eradication finally swamping the voice of empowerment.

Problem

There are two distinct problems with apocalyptic as answer to the "help-we-need." The first is that its calculations for the end are always unfulfilled, and thus the "help-we-need" is always receding before us. Second, and more profound, is the criticism that apocalyptic essentially offers us the "help-we-need" by obliterating those in the world we find different objectionable. In doing so it undercuts the very premise of the Abrahamic enterprise, namely that God loves the world, all people—and not just "us."

We still need help.

10

Voices in the Silence

The Hidden History

In most English Bibles the last printed book of the Hebrew Scriptures is Malachi.

Malachi is one of twelve prophetic books referred to in the Vulgate (the Latin translation that dominated the Western church in the centuries before the Reformation) as the "Minor Prophets." This use of "minor" does not mean that they are less important in comparison to the three "major" prophets, Isaiah, Jeremiah, and Ezekiel. The contrast is merely one of length. Perhaps we should refer to them as the three long and the twelve short prophecies—although this labeling might discourage anyone from reading the long three. Indeed, in the Hebrew Scriptures the short prophecies all are gathered in one book called "The Book of the Twelve."

We have learned enough to be alert to redaction issues immediately. How was this short collection of twelve put together and with what general purpose? (In the Koran, for example, the chapters are called *suras* meaning "gateways." They are arranged in order from the longest to the shortest and, because of this, constitute a real challenge to the first-time reader who might look for a historical pattern.)

The various books in the collection "The Book of the Twelve" cover a five-hundred-year period. (They seem to be gathered into some sort of chronological order in the Hebrew Scriptures. The compilers of the Septuagint departed from this and grouped the twelve books according to their comparative size. Ecclesiasticus 49:10 refers to Isaiah, Jeremiah, Ezekiel, and "the twelve prophets" thereby establishing a date by which the collection existed as such. This was probably around the third century BCE.) Malachi was a prophet of uncertain identity who lived at the time of Ezra and Nehemiah. I say his identity was uncertain because the Hebrew word *malachi* is generic, meaning "my messenger." While the title might have been given to a contemporary of either Ezra or Nehemiah, it might also have referred to Ezra himself. In any event, because Malachi is placed last in our printed Bibles, we often mistakenly make the assumption that it was the last Old Testament book to be written. Malachi is dated around 450 BCE. This means, for Christians, that there is an enormous period of biblical silence—nearly five hundred years.—before we begin to hear of Jesus.[41]

This five-century silence is broken, however, in two ways.

First, Malachi is not in fact the last book of the Hebrew Scriptures to be written and collected. That distinction almost certainly goes to Daniel, which we have already encountered in our brief examination of apocalyptic. You will recall that we placed Daniel (certainly its second part, chapters 7–12) in the Greek period, during the rule of Antiochus Epiphanes. Thus, we hear a voice in the middle of the second century BCE. We have cut the apparent silence by over half.

Second, during the two hundred or so years from Daniel to Jesus things were still happening, and books were still being written. (*Historie* and *Geschichte* continued.) Jewish life did not draw to a halt. Several significant events and turns of events took place. It is terribly sad that many who seek to understand Jesus fail to take into account his immediate past, the two hundred years we have identified. This failure is bound to obscure our interpretation of Jesus. How can it be that the two centuries of history, religious development, theological adventure immediately before Jesus' birth are ignored in favor of the time, say, of Moses as an interpretative key. Moses lived some two thousand years before Christ. It makes little sense.

The story of Jesus and its impact on his contemporaries remains obscure without some comprehension of the "silent period."

From this rich and complex time, I want to isolate four key moments or movements that had a profound impact on first-century Judaism, coloring the faith and the social environments of the people in the days of Jesus of Nazareth. In them, we can continue to hear voices offering the "help-we-need."

As we shall see, this period was far from silent.

The Septuagint

By the time of the early third century BCE a large population of Jews lived in Alexandria, Egypt, not far from the site of modern-day Cairo.

Alexandria had been built on the site of an older village by order of Alexander the Great and it was one of the most important and influential centers in the ancient Mediterranean world. At its harbor entrance stood a magnificent lighthouse, one of the seven wonders of the ancient world (the others being the colossus or huge statue astride the harbor at Rhodes, the statue of Zeus at Mount

Olympus, the temple of Artemis at Ephesus, the Great Pyramid of Giza, the hanging gardens of Babylon, and the mausoleum at Halicarnassus.) The city housed one of the greatest libraries in the world, the fate of which is lost in legend but which seems to have been destroyed in a fire in the third or fourth century CE.

At the beginning of the "silent period" we are looking at, Alexandria was home to a large Jewish population. The Jewish infiltration to Alexandria very probably began from Judah and Jerusalem as the Babylonians advanced in the sixth century BCE prior to the Exile. The route to Egypt was arranged as an escape for Jeremiah at that time—a journey that he refused to take. By the middle of the third century BCE most of Alexandria's Jews had been born and raised in Egypt where (in accordance with Alexander's Hellenizing policies) Greek was the language of the day. As a result Hebrew became the language of a select few, and was restricted to worship and study. Naturally amongst the large Jewish population there arose the need for a Greek translation of the Hebrew Scriptures.

Who undertook the translating work and when exactly it was done are now lost in time, but the preface to one of the books in this Greek translation, Ecclesiasticus, refers to the task nearing completion. Scholars believe this passage dates from 132 BCE.

One part of the legend surrounding this translation claims that seventy translators accomplished the project in a single sitting. It is because of this that the end result of their work is referred to as "The Septuagint," from the Greek for "seventy." The book is often referred to in writing by its Roman numerals, LXX.

The Septuagint shows us that voices were still being heard, and spoken, down to the early second century BCE.

It is worth noting, by the way, that for these people *translation was an acceptable way to hear the voice of God.* Some religions insist that holy books cannot be translated, that language and terms must always be retained "in the original." This is not part of the biblical mindset. Translation of the Scriptures is both acceptable and necessary. The translator is simply continuing the inspired work of communication. So indelible has this principle become that in English we almost invariably use the LXX titles for the books of the Hebrew Scriptures. Genesis, for example, derives from the Greek word for "origin" rather than from the Hebrew, *bereshith*; Deuteronomy comes from two Greek words that together mean "second law' rather than the Hebrew, *devarim*. We still hear the LXX voice.

Here is the key thing to realize and remember about the Septuagint. At the time it came into being (between, let us say, 230 and 130 BCE) the books of the Hebrew Scriptures had not been settled in any final sense. There were, of course, the books of *Torah* (the Law)—Genesis, Exodus, Leviticus, Numbers, and Deuteronomy. Also the great history and prophetic books had been collected into a group known collectively as *Neviim* (the Prophets)—Joshua, Judges, Samuel, Kings, Isaiah, Jeremiah, Ezekiel, and the Twelve (Hosea, Joel, Amos, Obadiah, Jonah, Micah, Nahum, Habakkuk, Zephaniah, Haggai, Zechariah, and Malachi.) These two great collections were, as we have already noted, finally redacted during the period of the Exile. Many other books which we now find in the Hebrew Bible were not as yet regarded as scriptural—Psalms, Proverbs, Job, Daniel, Ruth, Esther, and others.[42] That is to say, when the LXX translators began their job the first thing they had to decide was which books to include. There was no set notion of a closed group that was definitely "it." Things were still open. *God's voice (giving the "help-we-need") could be heard in many places.*

Also, the translators felt free to change the order in which the books were to be placed. In the Hebrew Scriptures, for example, Ruth is found towards the end between Song of Songs, and Lamentations. (These three, plus Ecclesiastes and Esther, are part of a small collection called the Five *Megilloth*, or the five "little scrolls.") In LXX, however, Ruth is taken out of the "Five" and placed right after Judges because of the book's opening words, "In the days when the judges judged." The translators were aiming for some kind of chronological organization. They also changed, to give another example, the order of the three great books of wisdom. In the Hebrew their order is Psalms, Proverbs, and Job. In the LXX it is Job, Psalms, and Proverbs—the normal order in English Bibles. More sounds of the LXX voice.

Accordingly, in addition to the *Torah* and *Neviim* the LXX translators included all the other books we now have in the Hebrew Bible *as well as some others* that were familiar to and loved by their community. I referred above to Ecclesiasticus. This is not a misspelling of "Ecclesiastes." Ecclesiasticus is another and very different book, one of the LXX additions. Others are Tobit, Wisdom, Judith, Susanna, Psalms of Solomon, and 1, 2, (and in some LXX versions 3, and 4) Maccabees.

In all there are in LXX two types of "additional books." First, there are the thirteen books that would finally, many decades later, become part of the Hebrew Scriptures comprising its third section (the *Ketuvim*)—Psalms, Proverbs, Job, the Five, Daniel, Ezra, Nehemiah, 1 and 2 Chronicles. Second, there are books that would, again many decades later, be *intentionally rejected* as part of the Hebrew Scriptures because there existed for them only the Greek and no original Hebrew manuscripts—1 Esdras, Judith, Tobit, 1, 2, (and sometimes 3, 4) Maccabees,

Odes, Ecclesiasticus, Psalms of Solomon, Baruch, Letter of Jeremiah, Susanna, and Bel and the Dragon.

These additional books are richly varied, including, for example, profound insights in the tradition of the Wisdom literature, as in Ecclesiasticus and the Wisdom of Solomon; informative history, as in 1, 2 Maccabees; and inspiring adventures, as in Judith, Susanna, and Tobit.

Some additional points can be noted.

For Jews in the Hellenized world, the Septuagint very simply was the Bible. Its influence upon the interpretation of God and God's will was deep and wide. Amongst these Jews were, of course, the early followers of Jesus who authored the books of the New Testament, the Christian Scriptures, and they were probably if not certainly writing in Greek themselves. Frequently, quotations in the New Testament from what is now referred to as the Old Testament can be traced, not to the Hebrew Scriptures, but to the LXX. Sometimes the importance of this cannot be overestimated. For example, In Matthew 1:23 there is a quotation from Isaiah 7:14. In English, the Matthew verse is translated something like, "Behold, a virgin shall be with child." In the LXX at Isaiah 7:14 we find the Greek word *parthenos*. This word carries the primary meaning conveyed by the English "virgin," although it also has broader meanings, such as "girl." The LXX translators used this word to correspond to the Hebrew at Isaiah 7:14, where the word *almah* occurs. The root word behind *almah* carries the sense of "ripe, ready, mature." It is almost invariably translated as "young woman." The notion of virginity may be implied in *almah*, but it is not primary. Reading the LXX *parthenos* connotes the primary sense of actual virginity, missing the primary sense in the Hebrew—the Hebrew, in fact, being the originating source. Subsequent Christian understanding of this translation has been profound, leading in some measure, with other influences, to the development of the doctrine of the Virgin Birth. In short, the "help-we-need" has clearly been heard, in the view of many Christians, in the LXX. And this voice comes out of the "silent period."

This is a good time to have a closer look at an aspect of biblical development, one that takes us beyond this period of the "hidden history."

In 70 CE Jerusalem was destroyed by the Romans. (More on this later.) With this came the subsequent dispersion of the Jews throughout the world (the Diaspora) and the accompanying loss of temple. It was urgent that parameters of religious authority be established as quickly as possible for Jewish identity to survive. A leading scholar, Yokhannan ben Zakkai, obtained permission from the Roman emperor, Vespasian, to gather students at Yavneh (or Jamnia, to give Yavneh its English form), a small town some twenty-five miles west of the ruined

Jerusalem. There, Yokhannan ben Zakkai and his followers began to reconstruct Jewish stability out of catastrophe.

Just as the crisis of the Babylonian Exile had prompted the collection of the *Torah* and *Neviim*, so too now one of the urgent questions addressed by the scholars at Jamnia was to settle what books comprised Scripture. Only then could they start to interpret God's will in their new situation—in the absence of their temple, in light of the Diaspora, and in the face of the power of the non-Jewish world. They had to choose. Would they include the additional books of the LXX, or not? They decided that, to be included, a book not only had to be loved and revered by the faithful, but it also had to exist in the original Hebrew. Further, the theologians at Jamnia rejected the LXX order of books and established a new three-part structure for the Hebrew Scriptures: *Torah* and *Neviim* (which already were part of the scriptural tradition) and *Ketuvim*, "the writings," which now included all those other Hebrew books noted above. (When abbreviated this three-part collection is referred to as TaNaK.) Intentionally excluded, therefore, were the Greek books included in the LXX, together with many others then in circulation. The Greek LXX books were to be "hidden away," which is the root meaning of the Greek word *apocrypha*. In essence and at its simplest, the Apocrypha is made up of these books.

This accounts for the existence of two Christian Bibles. Protestant Bibles include in the Old Testament only those books chosen by the Jamnia scholars, whereas the Roman Catholic Bible, the Bible of the Christian church up to the sixteenth-century Reformation, has its Old Testament the same as the LXX. (Some Protestant churches still include readings from the Apocrypha in their Sunday liturgy.)

Throughout the centuries of the early church there was always a certain uneasiness about these additional books. There was much debate as to whether they should be used to determine church doctrine. For our purposes here, however, it is important to note that through the added books voices from that silent period continued to be heard. Without them much of the immediate context for Jesus would have been missed.

Without them we would not have heard, for example, about the Maccabees, to whom we now turn.

The Maccabean Revolt

After Alexander died in 323 BCE, his last will and testament divided his empire into four zones. Each had its own governing authority, initially vested in four of Alexander's generals. Only two of these zones concern us. One corresponded roughly to ancient Mesopotamia and was governed by a general named Seleucus. Hence, this group can be referred to as the Seleucids; they were Hellenizing Syrians. The other corresponded roughly to ancient Egypt and was governed by a general named Ptolemy. Hence this group can be referred to as the Ptolemains; they were Hellenizing Egyptians.

Within a very short time, following the ancient patterns of geopolitics, the Seleucids and Ptolemains were competing with one another. Once again the holy land was caught in the middle of military struggles for world supremacy. The history of this time is complex, but the end result was the eventual domination of the Jewish area by the Seleucids.

The pressure on the Jewish population of Palestine under the rule of the Seleucids was enormous. We have already seen how this pressure found release amongst some through apocalyptic hopes, hopes that said something like, "Somehow soon, God himself will intervene and bring in a new age of victory for us and defeat for them." Others, as we shall see, caved in and collapsed under the pressure, abandoning the ways of the past to live as Greeks. Indeed, these "Hellenizers," as pro-Seleucid Jews were called, helped the authorities stamp out Jewish practices, and supported the high priests that were chosen by the Seleucids in violation of Torah requirements. Many others sought some sort of compromising middle way whereby they could preserve their Jewish authenticity while at the same time formally acknowledging the Seleucid masters and their culture. Still others fought back. These were the Maccabees.

How the Maccabean revolt started is fairly easy to grasp. Its consequences are more complicated. Let me sketch the main outline.

In a village called Modein an old Jewish priest, Mattathias, found himself facing a command to make a pledge of allegiance to the Seleucid masters. He resisted by slaying the official sent to enforce the new law. Mattathias then called for armed resistance. Since he was an old man, leadership of the rebellion fell to his son Judas to whom the nickname *maccabeus,* meaning "hammer," would soon be given. Many flooded to support the cause, no doubt due to the aggressive Hellenization policies of Antiochus (whom we have already met.) These policies can be exemplified by the "abomination of desolation" (Dan. 9:27) so called because it was so offensive to Jews. Antiochus had an altar to Zeus raised within the temple in Jerusalem sometime in late December 167 BCE.

Within a matter of years Judas's forces had routed the Seleucids from Jerusalem and had slaughtered many of the Hellenizing Jews. So successful were they that they were able to rededicate the temple in a great eight-day-long festival now known as Hanukah. This celebration took place in late December 164 BCE—three years to the day on which the abomination had been set up.[43]

Over the next two decades the struggle continued until, under the leadership of one of Judas's brothers, Jonathan, a measure of stability was attained. By this time the Hasmoneans (the family name of the descendants of Mattathias) had gained control of the high priesthood. Under Jonathan's brother, Simon, and especially Simon's son, John Hyrcanus, the Hasmoneans further solidified their control by taking the throne for themselves. Thus, palace and temple were united in one person. Ritual and Power as answers to the "help-we-need" became one in a dramatic, hitherto unimaginable way.

This was deeply offensive to traditionalist Jews, who knew that only a descendant of David ought to sit on the throne and who also believed that palace and temple should be separate clusters of influence in society.

The history of this time is wildly complex, rife with murderous internecine strife, factional competition for power, and an uneasy awareness of a growing threat out of the west. All too soon the troubled and competitive independence achieved by the Maccabean revolt was threatened by the arrival of Rome's legions.

The Roman Occupation

When the armies of Rome arrived in Asia Minor in 64 BCE the Jewish state was involved in its continuing civil war. The Roman general, Pompey, knew that the stability of the empire demanded that such internal struggles cease, and so he entered Jerusalem in 63 BCE slaughtering some twelve thousand opponents of the Hasmoneans. This simple, though ruthless act, showed everyone that Rome was a different kind of world power. There was to be no messing about with Rome.

John Hyrcanus, the head of the Hasmonean family at the time, became Rome's ally and puppet. He readily accepted a dependent status, and Judea became part of the Roman Empire. The Romans reduced the geographic boundaries of Judea and incorporated it into their larger province of Syria.

Rome itself was not immune to internal strife and, indeed, after the murder of Julius Caesar on the ides of March (the 15th) 31 BCE, civil war broke out. A mighty struggle ensued between Octavius, allied with Anthony, against Brutus, Cassius, and the other "republicans" who had murdered Caesar. After two decades of struggle between and amongst themselves, Octavius emerged as the undisputed leader. He anointed himself Caesar Augustus and ushered in a long period of stability—the famous *pax Romana*. This gave peace to the Mediterranean world and all Roman territories beyond it.

Little Judea was caught up in all this mighty flow of events. By cleverly seeing ahead and positioning himself as an ally and friend to Caesar, Herod gained the Jewish throne. Herod was an Idumean, a descendant of Esau, Jacob's "hairy" brother, and far removed from the line of David. Nevertheless, with the support of Rome Herod ruled for over three decades, from 37 BCE until between 6 and 4 BCE.[44] He embarked on many hugely ambitious building programs, not least of which was a major expansion of the temple itself.

The pressure exerted by Rome was different from but in effect greater than that of the Seleucids. Because of the help given to Pompey by John Hyrcanus, the Romans agreed to recognize Judaism as a *religio licita*, a religion that was permitted within the empire. Jews were not required, as were all other conquered peoples, to officially acknowledge Caesar as god. Thus, while their political and economic life was under the control of Rome, Jews were free to express their faith as they sought fit. (As we shall see, this is of huge significance for understanding Jesus and the witness of the early church.) The entire atmosphere under Rome was of a new kind of enslavement to a new kind of Pharaoh. Rome's power, stretching over the entire known world, seemed absolute, total, and unending. In one way the Roman rule was benign, leaving the Jews alone to "do their own thing." At the same time the presence of Rome's absolute power was everywhere, serving as a constant and threatening reminder of Jewish impotence and ultimate subservience. There was always a line that should not be crossed and if it were Roman ruthlessness was total. Crucifixion was a common site.

The *Geschichte* of this period can be shown as an extension of the archetypal pattern of history already noted, in the "History" section. In terms of the promise to Abraham it must have seemed as though Judaism's capacity to bless "all nations" was a wistful piece of romantic nonsense. (See Figure 11 in the appendix.)

Jewish Factions

(See the illustration *First Century Factions*, Figure 13, in the appendix.)

As a result of Hellenizing and then Roman pressure, Jews in first-century BCE Judea found themselves drawn into different factions, each with its own emphasis. Roman power was so total and ruthless that options had to be found for dealing with it and living under it. Rome's lordship over Judea was, like the Exile before it, a profound crisis for Jewish self-understanding. Once again the Jews questioned how they could possibly realize the Abrahamic promise. Where is the "help-we-need" now?

Three general options presented themselves; to accept the status quo, to focus on a new age, or to live in hopeful devotion to the ways of the past. The first of these attracted two groups of people; the second attracted two more groups; while the third was embraced by a single group.

The first group clustered around the status quo was the Herodians. The status quo, of course, was just fine for Herod and those who benefited from his power. A king always has a certain degree of economic control, and this fact ensured Herod's support.

The second group clustered around the status quo was the Sadducees. Their power base was the temple and especially the office of high priest. Religious authority and influence can also have huge benefits. The law said, for example, that only unblemished animals could be used in sacrificial rites. The priests were the ones who declared an animal unblemished. If, therefore, some worshipper arrived with a bull or goat it would not take too keen an eye for a priest to detect a "blemish" and to offer an approved animal instead, always "for a modest sum." The priesthood also received the tithe support of the produce of the land. All this brought in a handy income. Some scholars believe that the name "Sadducees" was a Hellenized version of "Zadokites" and, if this is accurate, the Sadducees were descendants of Zadok the priest who, as we saw earlier, had been the Jebusite native priest in Jerusalem. Centuries before, when David conquered that city he had put Zadok in charge of the Jerusalem cult and reduced the Levites to the ministry of music. The Sadducees were eager and strong advocates of the hereditary high-priesthood.

Opposing the status quo were those who longed for a new age. The Zealots believed that the Roman occupation was so terrible and total that no truck could be taken with it at all. No compromise was possible. Rome was totally evil. Only a radical change could make Jewish life possible. Many who felt this way wanted to prime the pump and help bring about the new age. The pump was to be primed with Roman blood. The Zealots were dedicated to killing Romans. They sought to avoid large-scale military confrontation with the Roman legions.[45] Hit-and-run terrorist tactics were their order of the day.

Joining the Zealots in a longing for a new age were the Essenes. They totally rejected the Zealots' methods, however, opting instead for a literal withdrawal from the status quo. The Essenes viewed the temple and palace as corrupt beyond reform. They left Jerusalem and returned to dwell in the historic birth ground of the people, the desert. Many scholars believe that the Dead Sea Scrolls discovered in and around the ruins at Qumran, near the north western corner of the Dead Sea, derive from this group. These scrolls reveal an ascetic and highly apocalyptic mindset. The Essenes viewed themselves as the "children of light." They longed for the day when the "children of darkness" would be defeated. It would be a day of restoration for the glories of Israel.

Rejecting the status quo as corrupt and the new age as naïve, a fifth group formed around the notion of devotion to Torah as the ground of hope. They sought to bring the sanctity requirements of Torah, requirements that hitherto had only applied to the priesthood, to any Jew. In embracing them this group consciously resolved to live separately from everyone else. The Hebrew *parush* means "to separate" and so the Pharisees were the "separate ones." As well as bringing purity laws into the home they worked to apply prophetic ideals of justice to everyday life through legislative interpretations of Torah.

The history of the Pharisees is very hard to pin down. Much of what we know about them comes from later sources written explicitly in opposition to them. It does seem, however, that they were the group responsible for the fostering, the development, and later the writing down of the oral traditions.[46]

The Oral Law

As we noted above, Jewish tradition claims that in addition to the Torah (the written law given on Sinai) Moses also received a body of oral traditions. These traditions were the interpretations and applications of the written laws. Why would a tradition of this kind be necessary?

Consider, as an example, the written law that forbids work on the Sabbath day. Questions arise, however: Is a doctor permitted to work on the Sabbath? Is it permissible to cook on the Sabbath? Can a farmer milk his cows on the Sabbath?

Interpretations and rulings began to be made as the need arose, and these were gathered in oral tradition. The power of oral memory is almost forgotten in our high-speed, computer- and print-dominated culture. For many centuries, however, memorizing was the accepted mode of maintaining cultural identity. It is said by some scholars that Homer was a storyteller and that he was capable of reciting the entire *Iliad* or *Odyssey*. Memory is a powerful tool.

Interpretations of the laws differed and developed with the passage of time. As far as doing work on the Sabbath is concerned, for example, there was agonizing debate about work to help the sick. In the tradition, an example is given of a stone wall falling on a passer-by on the Sabbath. Would it be permitted to clear the stones? The answer formulated was that such work would be permitted up to the point at which it could be determined if the injured person was alive or dead.

If dead, the work must then stop. If alive, the work of saving that life could proceed. (The one commandment, or *mitzvah*, in Judaism that overrules nearly all others is called *pekuah nephesh*, the obligation to "save a life.")

The point for us to note is that while the written law "Do no work on the Sabbath" seems straightforward, in reality it is by no means so clear. It demands amplification.

Throughout the development of these traditions the objective was always to help maintain the heart and intent of the written law.

Such rulings and the reasoning behind them are called *halakhah*, a Hebrew word meaning "the way to go." *Halakah* is the way to go faithfully through life as an obedient Jew. (Differing attitudes to *halakhah* is what distinguishes today's Jewish "denominations."[47]) Not all teachers agreed about such *halakhic* rulings. Divorce, for example, was hotly disputed. Some leaders followed a famous teacher called Shimei who argued that divorce was permitted only by reason of adultery. Others belonged to the school of another great teacher, Hillel, who stated that divorce was justified by any reason. (Does this debate remind you of anything?) Hillel put it this way. A man may divorce his wife "even if she spoiled a dish for him" (Mishnah, Gittin 9.10).

Centuries later, around 200CE, these oral traditions (interpretations of Scripture's laws) would be collected and written down in a book called the *Mishnah*, meaning "teaching." Times continued to change, however, and soon the *Mishnah* in turn became the subject of further study, interpretation, application, and commentary. These subsequent discussions were also assembled, this time in a collection called the *Gemara*, meaning "completion." Together Mishnah and Gemara came to constitute the Talmud, meaning "study, learning." There are two Talmuds, the Palestinian and the more famous Babylonian, or *Babli*.

The Talmud, together with the Torah, became the foundation of Jewish life for over a thousand years.

By the way, the oral tradition embodied more than legal rulings. There were folk-tales, philosophical flights of fancy, riddles, parables, sermons, and theological speculations. This further body of oral tradition is called *Aggadah*, meaning "narrative." *Aggadah* seeks to explain and apply Scripture in such a way as to effect, not your conduct (which is the aim of *halakhah*) but your attitudes and your beliefs. *Aggadic* material is usually found in commentaries on biblical books called *midrash*, meaning "explanation." There are many *midrashim*. *Aggadic* sayings often take the form of epigrams, such as Hillel's famous dictum, "Do not do unto others what you would not have done to you." (Familiar again?)

What is the point of all this? We cannot be certain, but surely it is not unreasonable to assume that when we read these documents, especially the Mishnah, we can catch the sound of the Pharisees' voice seeking to offer the "help-we-need." Echoes of *halakhic* and *aggadic* voices can be heard in the words of Jesus. These voices were articulated early on and became loud and clear during the "silent period" before our New Testament begins. Their various arguments were swirling about the ears of Jesus and his contemporaries.

There is much to be heard in the silence.

11

Encounter

❖

(a) Mark 5:21–43; Luke 19:1–9; John 8:1–11; (b) Matthew 5:1–11 with Luke 6:20–23; Matthew 7:1–5; Matthew 7:24–29; (c) Luke 10:25–37; Luke 15)

Jesus Is Born

The Christian Scriptures (the New Testament) begin with four books called Gospels; Matthew, Mark, Luke, and John.[48]

What is a "gospel"? Is it a biography? If so, how can we reconcile the apparent differences amongst the four in their accounts of Jesus? Which biography is correct? Let me illustrate some of the discrepancies.

Just about everyone reading this book will know that Jesus was born in Bethlehem. Nobody can avoid Christmas these days. Its omnipresent carols are heard in every mall and shopping center. Amongst these rings out "O Little Town of Bethlehem." In Bethlehem today, sadly the scene of much Israeli-Palestinian conflict, stands the Church of the Holy Sepulcher. It is claimed that this church was erected on the very site of the birth of Jesus. That Jesus spent his first days in Bethlehem seems an established claim. What is far less certain is why he was born there.

Why was Jesus born *in Bethlehem*?

Luke 2 tells us that in the days "when Quirinius was governor of Syria" a census of the population was to be taken.[49] This census required everyone to travel to his town of origin. Joseph, who was betrothed to a pregnant woman called Mary, made the seventy-five-mile trip from where they were living, Nazareth in Galilee, down to a small village some six miles or so from Jerusalem—Bethlehem by name. When they arrived the place was filled with folks like themselves so that "there was no room for them in the inn." That night Mary delivered her baby. Luke makes no mention of a "stable," but he does say she laid the newborn in a "manger" or feeding trough. Luke's story includes the visit of the shepherds. After a week or so the family returned home to Nazareth in Galilee, after fulfilling all the requirements "of the Law" (Luke 2:39). These requirements included several separate actions somewhat conflated and confused by Luke. Jewish sacrificial law demanded that all first-born males be offered to God, but it also provided for a way to pay for the child's redemption. So Joseph and Mary had presented the baby in the Temple to redeem him as a first-born belonging to God (Exod. 13:2, 12, 15). (See note 29.) Also Jesus, as a new-born Jewish boy, was required to be circumcised on the eighth day (Lev. 12:3 following Gen. 17:12.) This last, the rite whereby the male child bears the mark of the covenant, is called *brit milah* (commonly referred to amongst Jews today as *bris*[50]). Luke also relates the rite whereby Mary presented offerings in order that she might be pronounced ritually clean following the childbirth.

So, why was Jesus born in Bethlehem? Luke says because of the census. It is almost by accident.

Matthew 2 tells a different story. He speaks about the visit of some strange figures called *magoi* from the east. He does not number them, but they come with three types of gift for the "one born to be king of the Jews."[51] The *magoi* are sometimes called "wise men," but revealing their purpose to King Herod was not a wise idea. "Excuse me, O king; we have come to find the new king." No king wants to hear this. Needless to say, Herod sent them on to Bethlehem with instructions to return and tell him where to find the newborn king. They journeyed on to Bethlehem, where they found Jesus and then "being warned in a dream they returned home by another route." Meanwhile, Herod realized he had been tricked by the *magoi* and immediately issued orders for his bullies to sweep into Bethlehem and massacre all the male babies and toddlers, two years old and younger. Luckily, Joseph had been warned in a dream about this and managed to escape with Mary and the "child" into Egypt where they stayed until Joseph learned of King Herod's death.[52] At last, they were able to return home. En route they discovered that Herod's son, Archelaus, had become king in his place. Nervous lest he, too, had been told about the birth of the *magoi*-announced king, Joseph decided to head north with his family—up to Galilee. They settled in Nazareth.

So, why was Jesus born in Bethlehem? Matthew says because that was his home and that Nazareth was an afterthought.

Perhaps, you might think, the other two gospels can help clarify the situation. Unfortunately, neither Mark nor John has a single word to say about Jesus' birthplace, nor anything at all to say about him until he was a man and public figure. We should note, however, that while they do not contain a birth story Mark and John both refer to Jesus in ways that indicate their view that he had been born. Twice John calls him the "son of Joseph" (1:45 and 6:42), and Mark frequently refers to his mother, brothers, and sisters.[53]

This little examination of the birth stories of Jesus (there is no single birth story) shows us that the intent of the Gospels is not biographical. We should remember one of the rules about sound reading. Never make a text answer a question it is not asking. The Gospels are not asking biographical questions. Their intent and interest lie elsewhere.

Most New Testament scholars believe that the Gospels were written several decades after the events they speak of. A standard dating for the four Gospels would be something like this: Mark, between 55 and 60; Matthew, between 65 and 75; Luke about the same time as Matthew; and John, anywhere from 85 to 95. This gap between the events and their being written down need not alarm us when we keep in mind the power of oral memory—something we have already noted above. But, scholars also link the Gospels with different geographical areas. Again a standard view would link Mark with the church in Rome; Matthew with the church in Alexandria; Luke with the church in Antioch; and John with the churches of Asia Minor, today's Turkey.

Whatever the actual details may be, these facts mean that the traditions behind the Gospels evolved in different believing communities, in different contexts, at different times, and for different specific purposes. No wonder they are different. It is very far from unreasonable, given these circumstances, to see how this or that tradition or story would be preserved here and forgotten there, emphasized here and downplayed there. Consider, for example, that the Lord's Prayer—recited by nearly every Christian every Sunday—is not found at all in either Mark or John. Is this because they knew the prayer and chose to omit it, or because they did not know it at all? Which strikes you as the more likely explanation?

Why am I laboring this point? For two reasons.

First, because apocalyptic savior figures were not born. They suddenly were seen in the midst of the hottest fire (Dan. 3:25), or coming on the clouds (Dan. 7:13), or wreaking bloody havoc. "Their bodies are crushed by the might of Thy hand and there is no man to bury them" as the Qumran War Scroll XI 1 rejoices.[54] However strange, odd, and miraculous the birth of Jesus may have been (to which we shall return) the Gospels' insistence on it is a strong hint that they are not to be read as affirming the apocalyptic voice. The Jesus answer to the "help-we-need" is going to be very different. If apocalypticism views salvation as a transformation of time (this age will be replaced by the age to come) and as victory for us (the children of light) over them (everyone else, the children of darkness) the Gospels' view, as embodied in the person and work of Jesus, is leading us in quite another direction.

Second, to stress that the Gospels have a view; they have an intention; they have an agenda. They tell us something with spin, as our culture would say. They are not neutral, factual biographies (as if any biography could be). The Gospels are the communal memory of different groups of early followers of Jesus, and they were written down for two purposes; first, to provide the church with an *evangelistic weapon* with which to engage in the spiritual struggle between the will of God and the ways of the world and, second, to offer an *educational tool* with which to inform the faith of the community of believers.

Can we then somehow summarize what it is the Gospels want to say about Jesus? In what sense is what they have to say a true voice offering the "help-we-need"?

We shall attempt to articulate the distinctive help Jesus offers us under three headings, corresponding to the three groups of readings given above. They are: restorative possibility; revolutionary promise, and radical power.[55] All these are forms of empowering encounter.

Before looking at this, however, it might be helpful to take note of an important relationship, that between miracles and parables. They are first cousins, if I can put their intimate relationship that way. Let me explain

The word "parable" comes from two Greek words, *para* meaning "beside" and *ballo* meaning "throw." (A ball is something to throw.) A parable is the use of words to throw something beside something else. Starting from the familiar and known (the world of the field, the kitchen, the road trip, sibling rivalry, and so on) the parable teller seeks to take the listener to an awareness of the unfamiliar and unknown (the world of the "kingdom of heaven," the world the way God intends it to be). The "kingdom of heaven" is shown to be present. A miracle story works with the same two worlds, the familiar and the unfamiliar, only it is couched in terms of action not words, and it moves in the opposite direction, from the unknown into the known. "The kingdom of heaven" invades or intersects the world of the everyday and becomes present.

Sometimes, therefore, it is helpful to read a parable as a miracle in words and a miracle as a parable in action.

With that in mind let us proceed to our three groups of readings.

Restorative Possibility

Mark 5:21–43

This passage reveals a favorite writing technique of Mark. He sandwiches one story into the midst of another, a technique that scholars call "intercalating." (I prefer "sandwiching.") In this case the story of Jairus's daughter (vv.21–24 and 35–43) is interrupted by the story of the woman with the flow of blood (vv. 25–34). First, let us look at the stories independently, and then we will look at them together to see if their placement together gives us further insight.

The salient features of the Jairus story can be quickly summarized.

Jairus was a "synagogue ruler." It seems that this title indicated a lay official in a congregation who bore some responsibility both for the building itself (rather like a Facilities Committee) and for arranging services (like a Worship Committee). The title does not indicate any professional role or expertise. Jairus was in no sense a rabbi. He lacked theological training but nevertheless was motivated by religious faith. He fell at Jesus' feet out of pain at his daughter's situation. She was at the point of dying, and Jairus was sure that this wandering teacher could help. He abandoned any sense of dignity and self-importance he may have had; instead he was in the dust on the road before a stranger. Jairus was at the end of his tether. *All other options had run out.*

Jesus response is non-verbal. There are no questions put to Jairus such as "What makes you think I can help? Who told you about me? What is your understanding of me and my ministry?" Jesus simply responds by going with Jairus. His response to need is *reactive action.*

On the way to Jairus's house, they are met by messengers with the news that the sick girl has now, in fact, died. Jairus is urged not to bother Jesus any longer. Jairus's last tether of hope has been severed. In response to his despair Jesus finally speaks: "Do not be afraid; only believe" (Mark 5:36). What kills faith is not doubt or timidity or uncertain commitment. What kills faith is fear. *The opposite of faith is fear.* Jesus' response to fear is *proactive assertion.*

The conclusion of the story is that Jesus raises the girl back to life. Mark pointedly informs us that "she was twelve years old" and that she was given something to eat. The girl had been *restored*, both to her self and to her family. It is not too much to say that life had been restored to Jairus as well. His entire encounter with Jesus was a life-giving experience.

The salient features of the woman with the flow of blood story can also be briefly noted.

She, too, was at the end of her tether, having tried various remedies and wasted her financial resources on useless cures. *All other options had run out.*

She, too, had caught wind of the power of this wandering teacher Jesus, and she, too, made the effort to draw close to him. Reaching through the crowd she touched his cloak and "immediately" something happened. Jesus' *reactive action* was total, sudden, and instant. The woman's cure was immediate also. Mark writes that she "knew what had happened to her," that is to say, her flow of blood had ceased. Notice how carefully Mark is writing this passage. As the woman "knew" so too did Jesus, "knowing...that power had gone out." This passage is not carelessly or casually put together.

What transpired next is crucial. Jesus turned and asked who had touched him. This question was so ridiculous in the context of the crowds that the disciples said so. Jesus persisted. He forced the woman to identify herself before him with everyone watching and listening. (Once again, we see *proactive assertion*.) She, too, fell at his feet and told him everything. Is Jesus being sensitive here? Is this good, pastorally? His intent was not to humiliate the woman but to identify her clearly, not to himself, but to all those who were watching and listening. Why? Because a woman with a flow of blood was ritually "unclean" (see Lev. 15:19 and 25). Her sickness was more than a personal medical problem—it was also a public issue. The religious community forbade her to enter its worship services. She was living a life of exclusion. By compelling her to come forward and publicly display her new state of health, Jesus *restored* her—gave her back her self and then gave her back to her community.

Jesus summarizes this in his declaration to her: "Daughter, your faith has *sesoken* you." *Sesoken* is a form of the verb *sodso*. It is variously translated in this biblical passage: "healed you," "made you well," "restored you to health," and "cured you." Elsewhere in the New Testament *sodso* is invariably translated "saved" and its related noun, *soteria*, is translated "salvation." (Luke 1:77; 2:30; Acts 4:12; 13:26; Rom. 10:10; Eph. 6:17; Heb. 5:10 are a few of many examples.) It is not unreasonable to suggest that this verse could be translated, "Daughter, your faith has saved you." (The choice not to use "saved' and "salvation" in this and similar stories is a clear illustration of the power and influence of the translator.)

Could it be that Jesus is suggesting that salvation is having a self restored to its self and then having that restored self, in turn, restored to the community? Does this not begin to sound an awful lot like the "help-we-need"?

Now let's consider the stories as a sandwich.

One curious fact is the odd coincidence that Jairus's daughter was twelve years old and the woman had had her problem for twelve years. It may be that this is a literary device to aid in Mark intercalating the stories, as is sometimes suggested. There may be more to it than that, however. The woman had a "flow of blood" problem, meaning a menstrual problem. She had suffered from it for twelve years, the time that Jairus's daughter had been born. Notice how the woman is called "daughter" linking her in some sense with the little girl, Jairus's "daughter." Notice also how the restricted group Jesus very intentionally allows in to the room for the miraculous raising includes, in addition to "those who were with him" (that is, his followers), the "father and the mother" of the child. This is the first mention of the mother. Or is it? Could it be that Mark is subtly suggesting that the woman with the flow of blood was the mother? In some sense, she and the daughter are at the very least spiritually linked; their problems are similar. The woman's exclusion from the community of faith is a kind of death. This leads to the next point.

The woman was a religious outcast whereas Jairus was an insider, a "ruler of the synagogue." The status of each was irrelevant, not only to Jesus but also in their ability to find a solution to their individual problems. Their current religious status was both irrelevant and powerless. The same single requirement was needed from each. This bottom line stipulation, Mark tells us, was "faith." Jesus told the woman it was her faith that had saved her and to Jairus he demanded, "Only believe." Faith is the essence of the matter.

What is this faith in Jesus that leads to Jairus, his daughter, and the woman receiving the help they need? For centuries we have been told that Christian faith involves believing in the saving death and resurrection of Christ. How can that be the case here? Jesus' suffering, rejection, crucifixion, and resurrection have not even taken place. It must be that "faith" means something different to Jesus.

For Jesus, at least in this sandwich story, faith is trusting in him—trusting that he can give the help-we-need and in response doing something about it with your own life. It is to seek and to seize restorative possibility.

Luke 19:1–9

The salient features of the Zacchaeus story can be quickly highlighted.

He is called the "chief tax collector," *architelones* in Greek. This obvious implication of this to English readers is that Zacchaeus was in charge of a group of tax collectors, that he was in some sense the boss. This is a misunderstanding. Apart from this occurrence, there is no evidence whatsoever of there ever being an office of *architelones* in first century Roman occupied Palestine.

The tax collectors of the New Testament are clearly a despised lot, but however much we may not like paying our income taxes it is not correct to identify the employees of our Internal Revenue Service with these New Testament figures.

Remember that Judea was an occupied country, part of the Roman Empire. The power in the land was Rome, and its government's needs were what determined the tax burden. The Romans, however, did not have a huge reserve of tax collectors in Italy to disperse all over the empire. Instead, they evolved a system that has been dubbed "tax farming." The way it worked was that an area of a conquered territory was divided up into tax districts. The Romans determined how much revenue they required from each district. They then offered up the position of tax collector in the district to the highest bidder. Once he was successful in obtaining the position, the tax collector could raise as much revenue as he was able to squeeze out of the people, provided he gave Rome what it required from that district. Anything over and above that he could pocket for himself. Most successful tax collectors came from the native conquered population. It is not hard to see why they were so despised.

Luke calls Zacchaeus the *architelones*, meaning the epitome of tax collectors, the embodiment of tax collector-hood. Zacchaeus was at the zenith of his profession and the nadir of his community's estimation. He was the worst of the worst.

Little wonder that he climbed a tree to see Jesus. Driven by curiosity, he ended up in a tree not simply because he was short but also to symbolize his exclusion from the community below. The archetype of successful tax collectors could not find a place in the midst of the curious. Did he fear for his safety? Perhaps he did. In any event he was not part of the crowd that day as Jesus was passing through town.

So, when their eyes met it is no accident—Jesus looked up as Zacchaeus was looking down—that Jesus commanded him to "come down" out of his tree of exclusion. Like the woman with the flow of blood Jesus placed Zacchaeus right back in the midst of the community.

What follows is truly astonishing. Not only did Zacchaeus pledge to return all the money he had cheated people out of but Jesus announced that he would go to Zacchaeus's house for lunch. The crowd was stunned. Jesus was embodying an anti-pharisaic spirit, the opposite of "being separate" (*parush*, remember?). The story is rounded off (Luke 19:9) with Jesus' bold and yet unmistakably clear pronouncement that "salvation" (*soteria*) has come to Zacchaeus "today." More, Jesus goes on to state that this exemplifies what his ministry is all about: "to seek and to save (*sosai* from *sodzo*)."

Once again, we see restorative power. Zacchaeus recovered his integrity by returning his ill-gotten gains and, through Jesus' acceptance, he was restored to his community. The chief tax collector is the poster child of what Jesus meant by "being saved." Once again, there is no mention of the yet-to-occur crucifixion, resurrection, and substitutionary atonement. Zacchaeus's faith amounted to his change of attitude and action in response to Jesus.

The entire story is of the empowering encounter.

John 8:1–11

Nearly all contemporary translations of the New Testament will include a footnote when they come to this story saying that the best and most ancient manuscripts do not include it. Without raising the issue of its historical authenticity, therefore, I do want to suggest that it is an authentic Gospel story, in the sense that it summarizes what we have already detected in our Mark and Luke passages.

The woman brought before Jesus has been caught "in the very act" of committing adultery. Think about that. How do you catch someone "in the very act?" Who caught her? Was she set up? Where is the man? Has he been part of the set-up and so allowed to slip away? We do not know the answers to any of these questions, but if we are concerned so surely must Jesus have been. His subsequent behavior seems to reflect this. His *uneasiness with the accusers* is clear. (This uneasiness echoes a fundamental of the entire message of Jesus—the principle of reciprocity, about which more below, and its corollary, the urgent commandment not to judge one another.)

Yet, the woman does not deny the charge. She is *guilty* and as such by law merits the punishment. She should be stoned to death. For all practical purposes her life is over.

There follows a delaying tactic of Jesus. He writes in the sand. (How I wish I knew what he wrote. Many speculate, but nobody knows.) Then he invites the accusers to begin the execution if they are without sin. Jesus' clear meaning is that only the sinless can judge. Faced with this, the accusers disappear—beginning with the more mature, more experienced, more ashamed. Jesus and the woman are left alone.

What an odd contrast this scene is. The woman with the flow of blood was forced into the midst of the crowd. Here the crowd is forced to leave the woman caught in adultery alone with Jesus. This is pure encounter.

Jesus forgives her. This surely is what not condemning the guilty must mean. He sends her on her way to "sin no more." She, too, has been restored. She has been given back her life, literally, and given a second chance to live with integrity amongst her fellow human beings.

Once again we see the power of restorative possibility. As in the case of Zacchaeus Jesus summarizes what has transpired, but now he uses a very different vocabulary, one typical of John's gospel. He speaks of being the "light of the world" and of those he restores to self and community as having "the light of life." Note that Jesus intends the "lost," those who are walking in "darkness," to have life and to have it *now*—in the present. Once again, there is no sense that he intends everything to be postponed until some future death, resurrection, and atonement has taken place.

This is salvation talk in another guise. It is empowering encounter.

Revolutionary Promise

Matthew 5:1–11 and Luke 6:20–23

These are the famous "beatitudes." They have nothing to do with happiness. They are certainly not, as one book would have it, the "be-happy attitudes."[56] There is nothing happy about being poor, about mourning, about hunger and thirst. The root of the word "happiness" is "hap." "Hap" is an old English word meaning "chance." An old-fashioned word for an accident is "happenstance." Thus, happiness is something that comes by accident, always in the company of or as the result of other things, for example, doing the right thing. The American Declaration of Independence roundly asserts "life, liberty, and the pursuit of happiness" as "inalienable rights" bestowed by God. Happiness is something to be pursued but not guaranteed. To a certain extent it comes by chance.

Not so with "blessedness." Very simply put, to be blessed is to be approved of by God.

When athletes, actors, and others with exceptional talent celebrate their own excellence by saying "I am so blessed" they may be guilty of taking the Lord's name in vain, or at least of exaggerating his involvement in their lives. A God-given talent or gift does not necessarily qualify for the approval by God of which biblical blessedness speaks. Whom does God bestow his blessing on? That is the question Jesus' Beatitudes are intended to answer. They amount to a revolution in our way of thinking. Missing from the list of those blessed are the superbly talented, the outstanding achievers, and even the religiously enthusiastic, who also have a tendency to claim they are "so blessed."

So, who are the blessed? Let's list them: the poor, the mourning, the meek, the hungry, the merciful, the pure in heart, the peacemakers, and the persecuted. This does not constitute a list of society's happy people. But these, Jesus says, are those approved of by God.

More than that, the blessed receive promises: they will inherit the kingdom of heaven, be comforted, inherit the earth, be given satisfaction, mercy, and a vision of God himself. In short, to be blessed means not only that God approves of you but that he will give you all the help you need to become the person he wants you to be.

This is a radical kind of promise; it calls for a complete change in how society measures value and success. In the Beatitudes we hear Jesus teach, as distinct from seeing him in action, but the fundamental outline remains the same. He offers the blessed a promise, a promise that their fortunes will be radically reversed—and this is a form of salvation. Once again, prophetic themes can be detected: life as it is will be transformed and become life as it ought to be.

Matthew 7:1–5

The parable of the plank in my eye and the speck in yours is told to hammer home the essential principle: Do not judge one another. It is accompanied by a warning. If you do judge, the standard you use will be that by which you, in turn, will be judged.

If ever there was an ignored saying of Jesus this is it. Its companion, "Love one another," is also widely ignored. Christians have burned one another at the stake and continue to burn one another with their talk. (For example, I have always been troubled by the phrase used by some churches and fellowships, "whole gospel." The implication is clear. Those Christians who do not agree with them have only a "partial gospel" and, of course, the part, not being the whole, has no saving power. Partial-gospel Christians are doomed. That is the implication—and it is a very good model of how Christians judge one another instead of loving.)

The principle Jesus is articulating is the *principle of reciprocity*, heard also in the Lord's Prayer, "forgive us…as we forgive." This principle is intended to wipe out hypocrisy. A hypocrite is an "actor," the meaning of the Greek word, someone who pretends, whose entire life is a pretence, whose outer persona masks the inner true character. The principle of reciprocity is a summons both to compassion (for you may be as weak or sinful as the one you are judging) and discernment (for the actions you find offensive may not be identical to the one committing them.) Moral discernment, encouragement, correction, and exhortation remain part of the believer's duty—but not judging.

Jesus' plank-and-speck illustration, with its principle of reciprocity, shows us once again what drastic changes he demands from society in the way it operates on a day-to-day basis. Once again, we can hear the voice of revolutionary promise, namely that life lived Jesus' way will be better.

Matthew 7:24–29

The parable of the two houses, one built on rock and the other on sand, is easily misread. It is not that the house built on rock has an easier time of it. A careful reading reveals that the essential difference between the two houses involves a difference in commitment, equality in circumstance, and a distinction in outcome.

- The house built on sand is erected by someone looking for the easy way.
- Both houses suffer the same blast of wind and waves.
- Only one house endures; the house built with dedication, difficulty, sacrifice.

It may seem that the radical promise inherent in the teachings of Jesus we have just sketched is not worth it; that it calls for too much effort of heart, mind, will, and body; that it seems to defy pure commonsense. How much easier simply to "go with the flow" of culture and get by with life as it comes.

The revolutionary nature of Jesus' way is accompanied by the totality of the promise. The house built on rock (a life erected upon and devoted to his way of seeing things) will endure. This is not unlike John's "having life" or the vocabulary of *soteria*. This is nothing less than the "help-we-need."

Very well, you may be thinking to yourself, I will build the house of my life on rock. Pity about all those whose lives are built on sand. This is in no way an accurate reflection of how Jesus wants us to conduct our lives, as we shall shortly discover.

Radical Power

Luke 10:25–37

The parable of the Good Samaritan is so well known that I hesitate to mention how often it is misunderstood and its power missed.

In the parable we hear of two men whose lives are totally constructed on the sand of religious pride, convenience, and ritualistic formalism. We also hear of another whose life is built on the rock of discerning and committed compassion. So much is clear. Yet there is so very much more to this story than this.

Jesus tells the parable in a very specific context. A lawyer (an expert in Torah and *halakah*) had questioned Jesus about what he had to do to gain eternal life, that is to say, to get the "help-we-need," to be saved. Jesus turned the question back on him, asking him what he thought as an expert in Torah. The man replied with words from Deuteronomy 6:5 and Leviticus 19:18, possibly echoing an early form of the Jewish Sh'ma (the closest Judaism comes to a formal creed, a combination of the following passages: Deuteronomy 6:4–9; 11:13–21 and Numbers 15:37–41). The words proclaim a total love for God and a commitment to love one's neighbor as oneself.

Notice Jesus' reply. "You have answered rightly; do this and you will live."[57] The lawyer was still wanting to debate with Jesus, however, and, trying to show that such confessions of faith were glib and irrelevant, he further asked Jesus, "And who is my neighbor?"

This question is the context for the parable. It triggers the story. The question needs an answer. Who is the neighbor I am to love?

The answer that the parable gives is *not* the poor man beaten by the side of the road; the needy beggar you bump into on the corner; the world's poor and oppressed. Certainly they are people in need and neighbors in some sense, but that is not the parable's focus.

When Jesus had finished telling the story of the inconsiderate priest and Levite and the Good Samaritan, he turned to the lawyer and asked, "So which *of these three* was neighbor to the man who fell among thieves?" The correct answer, given by the lawyer, is, "He who showed mercy on him."

Who is my neighbor? Who I am to love as myself? The parable answers: the Good Samaritan.

What can this possibly mean?

Jews and Samaritans hated each other. As we have seen, the Samaritans were the remnants of the intermarried survivors of the Assyrian conquest of the northern kingdom. They had developed their own traditions and accepted as their Scriptures only the written Torah, rejecting as foreign to them the entire structure of Davidism and prophecy, wisdom, oral traditions, and the rest. They had created their own temple rituals and drifted far from Jewish life. Far from Jewish life, but living in the neighborhood. Samaria lay between Judea and Galilee—right on the doorstep of the Jewish community. There was so much hatred and resentment between Jews and Samaritans that many Jews, in traveling between Galilee in the north and Judea in the south, preferred to cross over to the east bank of the Jordan and travel in gentile territory rather than take a direct route through Samaritan country. Jews and Samaritans were enemies—intellectual, spiritual, emotional, and social.

Love my neighbor? Who is my neighbor? The Good Samaritan. Your neighbor is anyone who lives the life of humanity and compassion *even if* in every other respect you are conditioned to hate him.

In this parable Jesus is going way beyond the morally obvious injunction to help those in need. He is commanding love of those we would prefer to hate.

As the "help-we-need," such love is offered as a radical power. It saves.

Luke 15

Three types of loss are articulated in this chapter: a sheep lost through its own ignorance; a coin lost through its owner's carelessness; and a son lost through his own self-centered stupidity. Each is found (saved) by a total kind of dedication. The shepherd gives up all other tasks to find the sheep. The woman turns her house upside down to find the coin. The father wisely waits and waits and then rushes to welcome the returning son. The shepherd's searching and the woman's sweeping are both active love. The father's waiting is far more difficult—a passive, permissive, patient, and painful love.

The three are united also in the response to the finding again of the sheep, the coin, and the son. Most famously, in the parable of the prodigal son, a party is held. The "fatted calf" is slaughtered for a feast. But, the same note is sounded in the other two examples. The shepherd calls his friends and neighbors together for a celebration (a supper very probably not of roast lamb.) and the woman, too, summons her friends. The key is the rejoicing at the return of the lost. Jesus drives the point home: "I tell you that in the same way there will be more rejoicing in heaven over one sinner who repents than over ninety-nine righteous persons who do not need to repent" (Luke 15:7). I do not think we need to speculate about whether Jesus is here suggesting that a huge percentage of people do not need to repent. His point is clear. Heaven rejoices when a sinner repents.

Three common characteristics then can be identified in these three stories: loss, dedicated seeking, and joy at discovery. All three are further examples of the saving power of this new, radical, empowering, encountering love Jesus advocates and exemplifies. This salvation brings joy in heaven. It is the point. It is the "help-we-need."

Summary

In all the stories we have looked at under the three headings there is something missing.

How do the stories end? Did the woman commit adultery again? Did Zacchaeus resign his position and go on to live a righteous life? Did the lawyer find himself changed by Jesus' challenge to love his enemies? It is like wondering how Lazarus got on after he was raised from the grave. How and when did he finally die again?

In all this there is only open-ended possibility. The rest of the story is up to the individuals who were confronted and touched. Jesus summons us here and now to do something with our lives.

The capacity of the individual response is never swept aside in encounters with Jesus. Indeed, in the story of the rich young man, found in Matthew 19:16–22,

Mark 10:17–22, and Luke 18:18–25, the confronted individual turns away—a life challenged but unchanged. It is the only story of such a failure in the Gospels, but it illustrates the important point of individual responsibility.

This is both the glory and the weakness in the way of salvation Jesus enacts and offers. In the end it is up to us. Jesus is the Incarnation Principle present for us now. He offers wholeness of self as a radical possibility.[58] Jesus offers the empowerment of encounter. Jesus makes real here in our moments the power of *ehyeh asher eheyh.*[59]

Is this enough, or do we still need help? Is this enough or does the world which is the focus of the Abrahamic promise still need help? Has the scope of chesed been realized? Surely "my" encounter with Jesus is meant to be carried on until "all peoples are blessed."

How is all this to be done?

(There is no illustration of this Voice in the appendix. Instead, look in a mirror.)

12

Escape

✦

(a) John 14; Acts 6–7 (b) Romans 5:12–6:14; 1 Corinthians 15 (c) 2 Corinthians 4–5:10; Ephesians 1:3–14 and 2:1–10)

If the message of Jesus can be summarized as the Incarnation Principle present for me now—as *eheyh asher ehyeh* here in my now—and if in turn the realization of this in some sense depends on my response, several questions immediately spring to mind, amongst which are these three.

1.   What if my response is inadequate, falls short, comes and goes? What if I fail?

2.   Even if my response is authentic and continuous, what happens when I die? Is the promise meant for *now*, and that's it? Is salvation to be understood entirely as my authentic living in response to the empowering encounter of Jesus?

3.   If the key to my salvation is somehow encountering the restorative power of Jesus, how can I do that so many centuries after his birth? Where can I meet him now?

Let us come at these questions slowly.

Going to Heaven?

Heaven, as a place to go after you die, is an idea we have not yet encountered in our attempt to hear the biblical voices. This is hardly surprising. In essence, all the voices we have isolated are attempts to offer the "help-we-need." Our need is to be and become who we are meant to be here and now, so that all peoples in turn can become who they are meant to be here and now. This is the Abrahamic mission. *To suggest that the heart of the help is solely to "get to heaven" is in effect to abandon this mission.* The closest we have come to this type of response is in the voice of apocalyptic with its radical call for a new time that will blow away this present evil age and all who are satisfied with it. However, the apocalyptic vision is a time-based view. Going to heaven is a space-based view. The gospel voice, in insisting that "Jesus was born" and that the encounter with him is empowering, stands over against the fundamental dynamic of the apocalyptic point of view. What, though, about this going-to-heaven idea?

First, *the Old Testament (and Judaism for that matter) is not opposed to a life-after-death belief.*[60] In a rather beautiful turn of phrase, Abraham's death is described in Genesis as his being "gathered to his people." This suggests that there is a community of intimacy in the beyond and also that, in some sense, the individual will be able to enjoy the familiar community in the future. On the other hand, the references to Sheol are less cheerful. It is the place of the dead and is in some sense "below." True, the Old Testament declares that in Sheol kings still are enthroned (Is. 14:9) and prophets still are adorned with their mantles (1 Sam. 28:14), but generally speaking Sheol's inhabitants are weak and powerless, unaware of what transpires "above" (Job 14:21).

These Old Testament allusions are far from a full-blown view of the after-life. They do, however, remind us that the idea of life after death is not peculiar to Christianity alone. In fact, resurrection had become a matter of hot dispute between the Sadducees and Pharisees by the time of Jesus (Matt. 22:23–33). The key point of the Old Testament view, however, is that all the dead go to the same place. There is no distinction made between deserving and undeserving groups. There is, in other words, no "heaven" and "hell" in the traditional Christian sense. Where then did this idea come from, and is it a good idea?

Second, one of the most significant events in the development of biblical faith, and indeed in the creation of western civilization, was *the positive response of Paul to his vision of a man calling him to "Come over to Macedonia"* (Acts 16:9). Paul had been a persecutor of the early followers of Jesus who, in the famous incident on the Damascus Road (Acts 9:1–22), had experienced a "turn-around" and become an advocate of Jesus and an evangelist of the new faith. While his missionary tactic was first to enter the (Jewish) synagogues in the towns he traveled to in Asia Minor, he also reached out to non-Jewish pagans. (Some of these non-Jewish pagans are referred to as "god-fearers." This term indicates Gentiles who attached themselves in some way to the synagogue without undergoing conversion to Judaism—which tells us a great deal about Jewish attitudes to outsiders.

Such god-fearers were attracted by Jewish ethical monotheism in contrast to the pagan immoral polytheism that surrounded them. An example of such a god-fearer is Cornelius, as recounted in Acts 10.)

The vision calling Paul over to Macedonia was a departure—for him, Christianity, and the entire biblical enterprise. In responding to it, Paul was now plunged into Europe, into a Greek-dominated culture, amongst people for whom the message of Jesus as an embodiment of the Hebrew Scriptures would be incomprehensible and for whom the notion of the Abrahamic "help-we-need" was irrelevant. There was no point in Paul trying to persuade them with eloquent arguments from Jewish history. His audience had not heard of Abraham, Moses, David, the prophets, and the rest. Paul's challenge was to translate his conviction that Jesus was the center of life's meaning from Old Testament categories and Jewish images into concepts his Greek audience would understand, concepts that would intersect their lives and the structures of significance they had erected.

The chief influence for this audience was *the Greek view of reality*. For the Greeks reality was made up of two realms—this seen, transient world of actuality and another unseen, eternal world of purity. Needless to say, this view also carried within it a value judgment: the world of physicality was bad and the world beyond was perfect. Deriving ultimately from the teachings of Plato (or perhaps Socrates, to be more accurate) all this implied a spatial view of salvation. The idea was somehow to "get there," to the better, purer, less physical realm. How to do so?

In this view the knowledge of the world was essentially a form of ignorance and that such ignorance was a barrier to "getting there." Salvation, therefore, required a certain knowledge which, once obtained, became a ticket for the up-escalator to "heaven." Gnosticism (deriving from *gnosis*, the Greek word for "knowledge") was a philosophico-religious movement in the Greek culture that offered ways to obtain the right knowledge for this journey. This right knowledge was a form of *mysterion* or "secret" and was the rationale behind the so-called Mystery Religions that proliferated throughout the area at this time. Gnosticism was a major consideration for Paul's new audience and thus was a major factor in shaping his ministry.

The heart of the challenge before Paul was to translate Jesus as the Abrahamic "help-we-need" into categories the Greeks would understand. He needed somehow to present it with a spatial view of salvation, a value judgment on this world, and a need for a certain special knowledge.

Third, just as biology is a doctrine or theory about life (bios), and theology is a doctrine or theory about God (theos), so *Christology is a doctrine or theory about*

Christ. It is important to understand that in the pages of the New Testament we get the beginnings of Christology. The problem Paul faced, as sketched above, demanded that he develop and present the figure of Jesus in a way that would intersect the lives of his Greco-Roman audience and make sense to them.

One of the great questions of New Testament scholarship is the extent to which Paul knew or cared about the events of the life of Jesus. If the letters of Paul were all we had in the Christians Scriptures we would know virtually nothing of the man about whom Paul makes his astonishing claims. Paul is virtually silent about the things Jesus said and did as they are recorded in the Gospels, which, of course, were written after Paul's ministry. There are three possible explanations for this silence: (a) Paul did not know anything about these events; (b) he knew about them but regarded them as of marginal importance, or (c) he knew that others (he refers to "teachers" in his early churches) were communicating this information to his audience and so he could get on with his own work without feeling any need to rehash what was otherwise familiar. Scholars are divided. Some are of the view that Paul faithfully articulates the meaning of Jesus' life, while others find he "made up" the archetypal story of Christ and more or less invented Christianity.[61]

Fourth and finally, we have to observe that the Gospels themselves, not being biographical but driven as we have seen by spin, are engaging in Christological reflection themselves. Each of the Gospels implicitly offers a theory or doctrine of Jesus. Some radical New Testament scholars, such as those who constitute the Jesus Seminar, believe that very little in the Gospels can actually be traced back to what Jesus said or did.[62] Most of the material in them, the Seminar argues, is early-church spin. Others, on the very conservative wing of scholarship, maintain that we can turn to the Gospels with reliable expectation that we will hear the voice of the historical Jesus and see him at work.

The truth, in my view, lies somewhere in the middle. To argue that virtually nothing of the historical Jesus' words and deeds are to be found in the Gospels leaves me to wonder what then all the fuss was about. What motivated the early church? A will-o'-the-wisp? A mirage? What prompted the early Christians to live and, indeed, to die for their faith? A fiction? A vacuum? A nothing? I cannot believe this. On the other hand, to assert that all the gospel material takes us "back to Jesus" flies in the face of some obvious difficulties. These difficulties can be highlighted by what is known as the *Synoptic Problem.*

Let me try and summarize this problem.

It is based on two observations: first, that John's gospel is very different from the other three in style, tone, chronology, and contents; and second, that Matthew, Mark, and Luke exhibit a remarkable degree of similarity. Hence, the three latter are called the Synoptic Gospels because they can be looked at (optic) together (syn). These facts have become a marked focus of study for scholars in recent centuries.

The outcome of their work is far from universally accepted in all details, but its rough conclusions are now part of New Testament scholarship's standard assumptions. These are: Mark was the first to be written; Matthew and Luke used Mark or an early version of Mark; Matthew (the visit of the *magoi*, for example) and Luke (the shepherds, angel, and baby in a manger, for example) each had material known only to himself; Matthew and Luke together had material unavailable to Mark (for example, the Beatitudes, the Lord's Prayer); John was written some time after the other three and displays a more reflective mode of thinking about Jesus and a more intentional Christology (for example, the extended discourse, over four chapters, from 14–17, by Jesus about himself.)

Perhaps one or two illustrations would help.

Here is an example to illustrate the John/Synoptic difference.

In John 2:13–22 we read of the so-called cleansing of the temple in Jerusalem. In John's gospel he notes that this took place just before Passover. However, he also records two subsequent Passovers in Jesus' ministry. There is, of course, only one Passover per year. In other words, John's temple cleansing incident took place *three years before Jesus would be crucified.* In the Synoptic Gospels we read that Jesus cleansed the temple on the Sunday (now known in the church as Palm Sunday) just before the Passover *of the week he was to die.* In the Synoptics there is only one Passover. Jesus' ministry in the Synoptics is a one-year whirlwind experience. In other words, John extends Jesus' ministry over three years and places an event from the Synoptics' last week of his life three years earlier. In light of all this, some argue that Jesus must have cleansed the temple twice. However, not Matthew nor Mark nor Luke nor John makes this claim. John, with his three-year ministry of Jesus, describes several trips to Jerusalem whereas in the Synoptics Jesus makes only one such trip (with the exception of the boyhood visit told in Luke 2:41–52), and that is the journey which leads to the last week of his life, culminating in his death on the cross.

Here is an example to illustrate the Matthew and Luke dependence on Mark.

Read and compare Matthew 21:23–27; Mark 11:27–33; and Luke 20:1–8. They are virtually identical. Also, while Matthew and Luke are both longer than Mark, within and amongst them are many passages of almost verbatim correspondence. Of Mark's 606 verses all but fifty-five are found in Matthew, and of these fifty-five Luke has twenty-four of them.

Two formulas sum up these insights.

The Four Gospels = The Synoptics + John
The Synoptics = Mk + M + L + Q

> Mk equals Mark or an early form of it; M equals the material known only to Matthew, e.g. the visit of the wise men; L equals the material known only to Luke, e.g. the "Christmas story" and many famous parables, and Q (from the German *Quelle*, meaning "source") equals the material found in Matthew and Luke but not in Mark, e.g. the Lord's Prayer and the Beatitudes

John's Gospel provides a more intentionally reflective Christology than do the Synoptics. You will remember that in our outline of the possible dating of the Gospels John came last, somewhere between CE 85 and 95. Enough time had passed for the author to confront the need for a rationally constructed theory of Jesus, a sophisticated Christology.[63]

With this background to our three groups of readings we can now look at them more closely under the following headings: hope deferred; resurrection hope, and hope beyond hope.

Hope Deferred

John 14

This chapter is a part, the beginning really, of the long and extended farewell discourse of Jesus to his disciples. He and they are together in the Upper Room on the night of his betrayal. (Interestingly, in John on this last night together there is no supper of bread and wine, as in the Synoptics. Instead John and John alone reports the incident of Jesus washing the disciples' feet.)

Jesus talks…a lot….mainly about himself and his relationship with the "Father." Chapter 14 focuses on his departure to another place. This place is variously described, as "my Father's house," "(not) being present with you," "a place I am going to prepare for you," "being in the Father," "(where) you cannot follow now, but you will follow afterward," and "a place where the world will not see me, but you will." All this is far from clear. From a man who knows the physical agony he will face the next day, such opacity is acceptable. But, from an author writing some four or more decades later—is it acceptable? Is this Christology helpful? How does it possibly offer us the "help-we-need"? What does John (or possibly Jesus) mean by "there" as distinct from "here?"

The key in this chapter, it seems to me, is the notion of "the way." The chapter is dominated by spatial language. We are here together in this room tonight, but soon I will be there, where you all will arrive eventually, and this is the way to get there. Is that not the bottom-line logic of the chapter? I think so. In other words, the Christological claim is that the ministry of Jesus provides access for "his disciples" to "get there." The "there" is hugely undefined, but it is (a) where Jesus is going and (b) where his "Father" is. This has got to be good, right? We have hope "here" for some better "there." But is this not a mighty reversal of the "here" and "there" of *ehyeh asher ehyeh*? In that name God promises "here" to be always "there" for us. In this passage Jesus is leaving "here" and saying we will eventually join him "there," while promising to send from "there" a "Paraclete" to be with us "here." The desire to express things spatially seems to be straining the biblical witness. Also, this concept of the "way" is a very different from the root notion behind both Torah and *halakah,* both of which would have been very familiar to Jesus and his followers, and both offering a way to negotiate through this life of here and now. Is John now suggesting that such negotiation is either useless or impossible?

Acts 6–7

It may come as a surprise to learn that the single author who provides more chapters of the New Testament than any other is Luke. In addition to writing the gospel attributed to him Luke also wrote the Acts of the Apostles. This makes a total of forty-two Lukan chapters. Acts' opening preface (1:1–3) makes clear that the book is to be read as a supplement to the third gospel. Compare its preface to Luke 1:1–4. (This illustrates the confusing or at least unhelpful order in which we print the books of both the Old and New Testaments in English Bibles.)

One of the key components of Acts is the transition from the use of third-person pronouns, "she, she, it, and they," to first-person pronouns "I and we" at Acts 16:11. It comes immediately after "the man from Macedonia" appeared to Paul and, as we have seen, calls him over to Europe. Clearly from that moment on Luke, the author, was part of Paul's entourage and naturally speaks of "we" doing this and that. (Could it be that Luke indeed was the very man of Macedonia calling Paul to Europe? Most scholars are convinced Luke was a native Greek speaker. I think Luke is "the man.") In other words, and this is the point, the single greatest contributor to the New Testament was a non-Jewish intimate of Paul who, as we have seen, was impelled by the "translation necessity." This necessity would have been part and parcel of Luke's assumptions too, for he was a Gentile himself.

The story of Acts 6 and 7 must have been devastating for Paul to recount. Here we read of the stoning of Stephen. As we know, stoning was the punishment prescribed by Torah for blasphemy.

By the way, the assertion in John's gospel (18:31) that the Jews had been forbidden by the Romans to execute offenders is denied by this incident and by the "murderous threats" Saul the persecutor was carrying with him on the road to Damascus (Acts 9:1). It is also called in question by John 8:1–11 and by the repeated testimony of the Synoptics. What the Jews were denied, I believe, was the right to execute for any reason other than blasphemy or a religious offence of equal severity. They were denied the right of merely *political or criminal* execution. The Romans called this right the *ius gladii*, "the right of the sword." There is reference in the Talmud to this right being taken away from the Jews forty years before the destruction of the temple in CE 70. Josephus, a Jewish historian writing in the first century CE also makes mention of the right of life and death being put in the hands of the Roman procurator (*Wars of the Jews*, 2,8,1). The bulk of New Testament evidence is simply incredible if this right to execute is understood to have been removed for *all* causes. Indeed, the fact that the Romans executed Jesus by crucifixion was further substantiation of the political as distinct from the religious nature of his offense as perceived by Pilate. Caiaphas's concern was to avoid stoning Jesus for blasphemy which would in an ironic way have proclaimed that he somehow took Jesus seriously as a religious threat.

Back to Acts 6 and 7: Stephen had blasphemed, it was alleged, by speaking against Moses (the Torah) and the temple—saying they were unnecessary and obsolete. In his trial, testifying on his own behalf (which according to the Jewish rules for legal proceedings could not then be used in evidence against him, by the way) Stephen simply recited the Old Testament saving history and the prophets, coming to a mighty climax in accusing those who heard him of having rejected and killed "the coming Just One." Indeed, he went on, he could see Jesus standing at the right hand of God, thereby fulfilling precisely the promise we have noted Jesus made in John 14.

This broke his accusers' patience and in a fury Stephen was stoned. Those who did the stoning took off their coats and laid them at the feet of Saul.

Stephen was the first Christian martyr (*martyr* means "witness" in Greek,) and his stoning was a confirmation and exemplification of the meaning of John 14. The way to get "there" was to die, just as Jesus had died. (This surely is the intended meaning of the much abused text, "No one comes to the Father except through me" [John 14:6]. "Through me" equals "by dying." It does not mean, without a great deal of contortion and ignoring of the context, "No one gets to heaven unless you come forward at an evangelical meeting and murmur the Savior's prayer.")

The martyrdom of Stephen seemed to confirm it. We have hope "here" for some better "there." This incident must have had a profound impact on Saul, especially when later, now "Paul" after his conversion, he reflected on his new faith in Jesus Christ. It prepared him as no other event could have for his encounter with the Greek view of reality, with its severely depressing evaluation of life here and now.

Having hope "here" for some better "there" is hope deferred.

Resurrection Hope

Romans 5:12–6:14

In the space of these twenty-four verses, Paul uses the word "sin," in some form, together with "transgression" "offence" and "disobedience" twenty-four times. That is at the rate of once per verse. Additionally, he uses "death" or "dies" nine times. It is clear what is on his mind.

If our hope to get "there" from "here" is deferred until I die, two questions occur: why is this so, and, does it matter how I have lived my life? These questions point to the issues of cause and consequence.

To deal with the first question, Paul turns to the figure of Adam. It is well to keep in mind that in our examination of Genesis 2 we did not find the word "sin." The natural reading of the passage does not suggest Paul's interpretation. The influence of Paul's exegesis of Adam, however, has been indelible on subsequent Christian thought (as we shall see in *Speak Up—Faith Talking! an invitation to biblical living*, the companion volume to this book, when we consider the influence of Augustine.) Paul's argument moves through three stages.

Stage one establishes the *universality of sin*. The origin of "sin" is the offence of the first man. The implication in Paul's argument is that death was the result of Adam's disobedience. It would not otherwise have occurred. As he so roundly puts it in verse 21, ".... sin reigned in death." Since Adam was the one from whom all human beings came, the consequence of his action was universal. Our sin is original sin—sin that derived from the origins of humankind, irreversible by human effort.

Stage two establishes the *universality of judgment*. Paul writes in verse 18, "Therefore, as through one man's offense judgment came to all." Based on the merits of our lives we all deserve not only to die but to remain dead, if I can put it that way. By "all," Paul means all—every single solitary human being who has lived, is alive, and ever will live. Absolutely nobody deserves to catch the up-escalator. Nobody is going to make the trip from "here" to "there." Paul argues that we do not even deserve to nurture the hope deferred we have already outlined. This is a desperate situation and a thoroughly gloomy evaluation of human life, character, and potential. (There is no view here of Jesus saying, "Go and sin no more.") But, there is an answer to come, a bright hope.

Stage three establishes *the power and scope of grace*. Grace is more "abundant" (v. 20) than sin. Thus, in some way, grace can overcome the desperate consequences of sin. Grace can and does lead to that up-escalator after all (v. 20 says, "So grace might reign through righteousness to eternal life through Jesus Christ our Lord.") Somehow, this solution is bound up with what Paul calls Jesus' "obedience" in dying on the Cross and his being raised to life (see 6:5–7). The cross/resurrection mechanism needs some more explanation (which 1 Corinthians 15 will provide for us momentarily). For now, I want to focus on this grace and its extent.

Grace, first and foremost, is a "free gift" (5:15). Think of the dynamics of gift giving. The giver is in total control of what the gift is to be and when it is to be given. The receiver has neither control nor any say in what the gift should be (unless you live in homes where you can say what you want for Christmas.) A gift, by its very nature, is free in the sense that the receiver cannot earn it. If the gift is the result of effort then it is not a true gift but "wages," a due reward, and in some sense the giver is obliged to give it. A true gift, in contrast, is an undeserved treasure.

This is the key to understanding Paul's argument. He has argued that we deserve only death. In order to escape this situation we will have to receive something stronger than death that we do not deserve—a powerful gift. This, he states, is grace. (I liken grace to super-glue. Grace is the super-glue of the love of God; it is his love applied with such adhesion that nothing can shake it loose. Grace is a dynamic, active force.)

Who then receives this grace? If (a) sin is universal, (b) death is its inevitable consequence, and (c) grace is the only power that can bring escape from this consequence—who is to receive the gift?

Paul's answer seems clear: "as many of us as were baptized" (6:3); "we (who) have been united together in the likeness of his death, certainly we also shall be in the likeness of his resurrection" (6:5). The scope of grace is less than universal, Paul argues. It is limited to those who have been "baptized in Christ Jesus" (6:3).

Is Paul adding to the mechanism of grace? Is baptism now an additional and, in some sense, necessary step to completing the resurrection of Jesus? Does the power of Jesus' resurrection not apply without baptism? And what about post-baptism sinning? Does it disqualify or in some way rub out the grace? Is the escape from death in this mechanism Paul has described as fragile as our own moral resolve?

Is resurrection hope a reality or a rhetorical device? Is it really the "help-we-need"?

1 Corinthians 15

The entire point of this magnificent chapter is to argue for and establish the reality of resurrection hope. It is as real as the actual, physical, bodily resurrection of Jesus. This reality was the central conviction of Paul's life. It encapsulated his Damascus road experience, authenticated his claim to be an apostle, and impelled his subsequent life of evangelism. Without it Paul's understanding of the gospel is hollow; without it "our preaching is empty" (15:14). When he was preaching to the intellectuals of Athens gathered at the Areopagus, as recounted in Acts 17:22–34, he received a cordial hearing until he made the resurrection claim. At that, the crowd was divided, some remaining curious, and others mocking. The bodily resurrection of Jesus is, for Paul, not only an historical fact but also the essential escape mechanism. Without it there is no way from "here" to "there."

These central points from 1 Corinthians 15, together with more on Adam and Christ, echo in large part the passage from Romans we looked at above. (In actuality, scholars date Romans after 1 Corinthians.) However, in this passage there is a very different tone, one that directly challenges all we have hitherto heard in our examination of the biblical voices.

To emphasize the escaping ("here"-to-"there") power of resurrection, Paul has some disparaging things to say about life here and now. "If in this life only we have hope in Christ, we are of all men most pitiable" (15:19). Without resurrection hope, without the escape route, faith is "futile" (15:17). "There is a natural body, and there is a spiritual body" (15:44) and the natural body is the occasion of "corruption...dishonor...weakness" (15:42, 43).

It is hard to resist making two observations. One is that Paul has absorbed, or is at least catering to, a Greek view of physicality at odds with the rest of the biblical witness in order to persuade. The other is that Paul seems to be advocating a pie-in-the-sky-bye-and-bye approach to evangelism—by which I mean an evangelism that offers a postponed, post-death answer as the only "help-we-need."

Is Paul's argument and presentation truly tenable from the point of view of the biblical voices we have so far heard?

Is resurrection faith inevitably bound up with this salvation-as-escape mechanism?

Hope Beyond Hope

2 Corinthians 4–5:10

These verses again echo many of the themes we have already noted. Two new salient features are introduced, however.

First, Paul's gospel is not inevitably successful. Many do not receive it, turning their backs on the escape route. What happens to such folks? Paul describes them as "perishing, whose minds the god of this age has blinded" (4:3, 4). In short, the saving mechanism of resurrection does not work unless the preacher can persuade. Where the preacher fails, people perish. (This is a stunning reworking of ritual as necessary.) Is it possible that grace, after all, is not the strongest power there is? If grace can be resisted and rejected then it follows that it is as weak as the power of human response and resolve? (Compare John 3:16.)

We still need help.

Second, what about the conduct of the believer after baptism, after receiving the gift? Once saved, always saved? It seems not. Judgment "there" still awaits (5:10), and it will amount to a keen assessment of the believer's conduct. "Each one may receive the things done in the body, according to what he has done, whether good or bad" (5:10). This seems thoroughly at odds with what Paul had argued about grace, resurrection, and baptism elsewhere. He is at great pains in his letters, which scholars usually analyze as falling into theological and ethical sections, to urge right living upon his readers. He insists we live ethical lives with evangelical zeal. The journey from "here" to "there" carries an ethical and evangelical imperative. After all, the pie-in-the sky is not meant for me alone.

This seems at odds with his argument in the next passage.

Ephesians 1:3–14 and 2:1–10

The first section of this reading is a beautiful passage redounding with positive affirmation and underscoring many of the points Paul has made in Romans and Corinthians.

Many scholars believe Ephesians was not written by Paul but by a disciple or follower—someone deeply influenced by him. If so, this Pauline passage is reassuring. We might note, by the way, that it clearly enunciates the doctrine of predestination. God the Father "chose us in (Christ) before the foundation of the world" (1:4). Poor old John Calvin and the Presbyterians have been blamed for making this up. Note also the purpose of this predestined status: "...that we should be holy and without blame before him in love" (1:4).

The author summarizes the escape-route power of grace in 1:7–9. But then something curious is added. The Pauline author of Ephesians must have been uneasy with Paul's bare teaching on baptism and its potential exclusionary emphasis. He affirms the Abrahamic dimension of grace's intent: "That he might gather together in one all things in Christ, both which are in heaven and are on earth" (v. 10). This is a magnificent reaffirmation of the Abrahamic vision. "All things" are to be gathered. Surely the author intends us to understand that, indeed, grace is the most powerful force in creation and that a universal ("all things") embracing is God's intention.

The second section contains an astonishing description of the "there" to which God through grace will bring those "predestined." "(He) made us alive…raised us up…made us sit…." (2:5,6). These verbs duplicate in us what transpired in the risen Christ. In other words, where he went we shall go. Is this not what John 14 had promised? Our destiny is to sit with him at the right hand of God the Father. It is breathtaking.

But, wait. Without grace we are "dead in our transgressions" (2:5). What can a dead person do to help him or herself? Nothing. Only resurrection power can enable. Thus, even the human response, called faith, is a gift from God. "For by grace you have been saved (*sesosmenoi* from *sodso*) through faith, and that not of yourselves; it is the gift of God, not of works, lest anyone should boast" (2:8, 9).

Summary

Let us see if we have this.

The argument seems to be: (a) As a human being, a descendant of Adam, I am dead. (b) Being dead means not only that I will actually die one day but also that here and now I can do nothing to please God and to deserve his love. (c) God chooses to give me faith for some as yet totally unexplained reason. (d) Having received his grace, and having been baptized, I am "guaranteed" (1:5) a trip on the up escalator. (e) All I do after baptism, good and bad, is, however, totally relevant and will be used in judgment when I confront God the Father.

Is it too much to conclude: *We still need help?*

"All peoples" still need help.

13

Endurance

❖

(Mark 13; 1 Thessalonians 4:13–5:24;
Revelation 21)

Apocalyptic with a Twist

We closed the last section by expressing some uneasiness about the ethical dilemma faced by baptized, and thus "saved," believers in Jesus Christ. Somehow we are still going to be held accountable for our actions, even though without grace there is nothing we can do to gain or merit the love of God. This uneasiness can be expressed in terms of a riddle or conundrum:

* *Christ died to save me. Is it necessary that I believe this?*

If the answer is "yes," then it is not Christ's dying (and rising again and taking a seat at the right hand of God) that saves me in fact, but it is my act of believing it. There is a huge inner contradiction.

If the answer is "no," then my moral conduct and whether or not I "believe" in the here-and-now becomes irrelevant since I am already saved. (I will eventually be catching the up-escalator.) Once again, this implies a huge inner contradiction.

"Works righteousness" is a phrase often used to describe the view that how we live and how we act will, in fact, constitute whether we are saved. Our works, our actions in the here-and-now, carry saving potential. Paul was adamant in rejecting this view. In fact, he was almost in danger of overstating the case, leading either to (a) a kind of uncaring lifestyle, dubbed by scholars as antinomianism, an amoral indifference, or to (b) a withdrawn, quiet, retreat-from-the-fray kind of lifestyle. The letter of James is written, in part, to counter both these distortions.

"Faith without works is dead," James thunders (James 2:14–26). Works, *motivated by faith*, constitute righteousness.

The point is that, if we live in recognition of the ethical and evangelical imperative, works are enacted *not to gain the love of God but to express gratitude at having received it.*

The harsh truth of the matter, however, is that for the early church certainly, and for contemporary believers still, the world remains a thorough mess. Starvation, injustice, warfare, greed, selfishness, immorality, cultural shallowness, vapid art, innocent suffering—all these remain. Believers today may not face outright persecution, as did the early church, but they often find themselves surrounded by a culture of wild indifference, one going its merry way without so much as a quiver of concern about what the faith may or may not have to say about it.

In short, shot through the very fabric of salvation faith there is a polar tension between "already" and "not yet." In some sense, salvation is an "already" since the Christ event has occurred, never to be repeated. At the same time, "not yet" can we point to the fulfillment of the Abrahamic promise; "not yet" are all peoples blessed; "not yet" do all people—even believers—live in the image and likeness of God; "not yet" do all people live in sacred space and time. If Christ has already died to save the world, "not yet" has the impact become clear. It is one thing for us to believe "here" that after we die we will be "there." It is a very different thing for us to continue to put up with a world so radically out of tune with God's will. Surely, something will have to give—and soon.

In a sense, this restlessness is testimony to the fact that saving faith has to embrace more than what happens to "me" after I die. It is a reassertion of the Abrahamic insight. If biblical faith is true then somehow it has to impact the world.

The urgency is the very soil that nurtures apocalyptic, as we saw above. In it salvation is viewed not so much in spatial terms (of going from "here" to "there") as in temporal terms (the "now" that is so unbearable will soon, very soon, at any instant, give way to the "then" of peace, bliss, and victory).

It is not at all difficult to see how this urgency gripped the early church. A group of believers who "already" had received the "here-to-there" salvation message of Paul had still to face the "not yet" of victory.[64]

They needed to evolve a way of enduring this tension.

The readings itemized for this section show exactly how they did this.

Restless Urgency

Mark 13

Several crucial points must be kept in mind.

First, in Bibles that print the words of Jesus in red, most of Mark 13 is red (but not in the version of the Jesus Seminar.) The chapter is a discourse by Jesus, by far the longest in Mark and, excluding the composite Sermon on the Mount/Plains of Matthew and Luke, in all the Synoptics. This ought to raise a red (!) flag. This chapter is out of character with the Jesus we otherwise know in the Synoptics.

Second, the discourse is spoken in response to a question put to Jesus by Peter, James, John, and Andrew. In other words, it is teaching given to a few, not broadcast widely.[65] Moreover, it is teaching drawn out by means of their inquisitiveness. The heart of their question articulates what I have called apocalyptic restless urgency: "When will these things be" (Mark 13:4)? This is the heart of the apocalyptic mind-set. When?

Third, what prompted their question was Jesus' referring to the imminent destruction of the temple, which in turn had been stimulated by the disciples' admiration of it (13:1). Herod's temple, as it is referred to, was a much larger and more magnificent structure, with many additions and extensions, than the small building of the immediate post-Exilic period. (Some scholars refer to the period of Herod's temple, ending in 70 CE, as Third-Temple Judaism.)

Fourth, at this point we should pause and review the events of 70 CE, already mentioned. In that year four Roman legions, after putting up with zealot attacks and for years pleading with the Jewish authorities to put a stop to them, received the order to take all steps necessary to end Jewish uprisings. The Roman commanders responded, under the generalship of Titus, son of the newly proclaimed emperor, Vespasian. The result was the devastation of Jerusalem. There was a siege with its consequent widespread starvation after which the Roman soldiers entered the city. They indiscriminately slaughtered much of the population, destroyed the palace, burned and leveled the temple, and placed the Roman eagle standards in its ruins. The Romans subsequently issued an edict that banned Jews from living within the boundaries of the holy city. It was this that led to the Diaspora, the dispersion of the Jews across the then-known world. The extent and scope of this disaster upon Judaism cannot be overemphasized. Insofar as it occurred at a time when the relationship of the followers of Jesus to Judaism was not yet settled and there still lingered the idea that Jesus' followers were still in some sense Jewish, it was also a disaster for them. What sense could be made of it? What did it all mean?

If, as most would agree, Jesus died some four decades before these events in a social and political context that was, if not entirely stable, far less volatile than prevailed in 70 CE, how are we to read this chapter? Is it a prescient prediction by a prophet? Or is it an attempt to make sense of a disaster, either imminent or immediately past, by a small and threatened community?

In examining the Gospels we noted how they all, in their own ways, insist on the actual humanity of Jesus—he was born, had brothers and sisters, was known to his neighbors and townsfolk, and so on—and that this human rooting is in conflict with the notion of an apocalyptic hero-figure. Such figures came "out of the supernatural blue," as it were, in odd ways and with weird powers. But Jesus was born into a family, into the Nazareth community, and did not emerge as a public figure until nearly the middle or so of the third decade of his life. And even then he emerged as a preacher, teacher, and healer, not unlike many others. *What distinguished Jesus to his contemporaries was not his origin but the radical authority he claimed for the content of his message.*

Yet, Mark 13 seems to revert to apocalyptic images: cosmic battle and tribulation; division of people into the elect and others; an apocalyptic hero (the Son of Man as here entitled) coming on clouds.

The main thrust of the chapter, however, is clear and stands in marked contrast to the essence of apocalypticism. The disciples had asked "when." Over and over again in this chapter they are told to "wait," "take heed," "watch," "endure," "not be deceived." The chapter is going out of its way to say *not* to try and calculate when it all would be.

Did Jesus, some four decades in advance, actually predict the fall of Jerusalem in 70 CE? If so, this chapter is urging that the early church not think of it as some kind of apocalyptic end. They should endure and persist for the long haul.

Did the early church put these words into the mouth of Jesus after the events of 70 CE in an attempt to make some sense of the calamity? If so, the sense they are making is that 70 CE in no way marks some kind of apocalyptic end. The message is the same. They should endure and persist for the long haul. The chapter is a summons to endurance no matter how hard the way becomes.

If the "Son of Man coming on the clouds" is intended to refer to Jesus in any way it has to refer to him as coming after the Resurrection in order that his origin can meet the supernatural requirements of the apocalyptic hero. These are the seeds of what would become the full-blown doctrine of the Second Coming.

In any event, Mark 13 as it stands does not meet the calculating needs of the true apocalyptic desire.

1 Thessalonians 4:13–5:28

First Thessalonians was written by Paul before Mark's gospel was put together. Many scholars regard it as the earliest book of the New Testament, dating from about 50 CE. This is twenty years *before* the destruction of Jerusalem.

In our passage we hear Paul speculating about what he calls the "Day." Amongst Old Testament prophets the phrase the "Day of the Lord" had been used to point out that soon God would intervene and either wreak deserved havoc or bring longed-for relief, depending on the prophetic context. One of the clearest examples of this is found in Joel, the whole of which is an extended meditation on the "Day of the Lord." In the apocalyptic writing that comes out of the "silent period" between the testaments (as, for example, amongst the Qumran documents) this phrase had been widely seized upon to articulate the apocalyptic end-time vision. It was, in other words, a code word for the final battle and victory of "us" over "them."

In our passage Paul's clear intention is to use this image and its related notions to comfort his readers. This is made clear especially in 5:11, "Therefore comfort each other and edify one another." The need for comfort came from the disturbing fact that many of the disciples were dying and were thought, therefore, to have "no hope" (5:13).

Obvious from this passage is the confusion that reigned in the early church about the nature and timing of an individual's resurrection from the dead. It seems that Paul's readers were of the view that the apocalyptic end should take place before any of them died. Since some of them were dying before it then those left behind were concerned that their departed loved ones were going to miss out on catching the up-escalator, as spoken of in John 14. Paul writes to comfort them, saying that their worry is unfounded. When "the Lord himself will descend from heaven with a shout, with the voice of an archangel, and with the trumpet of God" then both those who were alive at that moment and all those believers who had died previously would be "caught up together" (5: 16,17). It is as if the dead were waiting in some kind of departure lounge from the moment of their dying until the Day.[66]

This notion is at odds with much Christian thought. Not least amongst the ideas Paul is at odds with is that contained in the later passage in Matthew 27: 51–53 (a passage not frequently preached from). Here we see that at the moment of Jesus' death on the cross graves popped open and, after the resurrection, the dead came out and walked about the streets of Jerusalem, being seen by many. As far as Matthew is concerned, the Day is a kind of combined Good Friday/Easter that has already taken place. Moreover, the Thessalonians passage is at odds with what Paul will later write in 1 Corinthians 15, as we have already seen. Establishing the here-and-now power and effectiveness of Jesus' resurrection, Paul writes that if it did not happen "also those who have fallen asleep in Christ have perished" (1 Cor. 15:18). But, this is the very group his Thessalonian audience had been concerned about and who Paul had earlier said would remain in the departure lounge until the Day. In 1 Corinthians Paul's logic clearly suggests that any journey from "here" to "there" will take place instantaneously. It is true that even in this passage from Corinthians apocalyptic echoes remain; he speaks of "the last trumpet," of being "baptized for the dead," and of Christ's "coming."

It seems clear to me that Paul's mind changed and his thought developed as it slowly became obvious to him and all others in the early church that the apocalyptic return of the Son of Man on the clouds to usher in victory and exalt "us" over "them" was not going to happen any time soon, certainly not this week, nor next month, nor even, very probably, in their lifetimes. So it is that Paul is at pains, even in our 1 Thessalonian passage, to urge upon his audience the moral and evangelical imperative, as in 1 Thessalonians 5:12–28.

The message is the same as Mark 13. It is a summons to endurance no matter how hard the way becomes. Once again, the heartbeat of true apocalyptic is missing.

Revelation 21

No brief account of Revelation can begin to do it justice. With that caveat, let me say that it is my view that no other book of the entire Bible has been so widely misrepresented and distorted in recent decades. It has been mined to find references to current, even daily, events; to minutely predict the "end of the world" (despite Jesus and Paul's warning not to do any such thing); and to calculate who actually will and who will not "go to heaven" according to the vocabulary of rapture, tribulation, and one or another form of millennialism. It is all very sad and flies in the face of the fundamental truths and sound rules we articulated at the beginning of this study. For now, let me simply state my view that Revelation is a book of theological poetry and as part of the poetry genre is never to be taken literally. To do so destroys the poetry. To understand it adequately we must read it with the book of Genesis side-by-side. Revelation's fundamental message is identical to that already outlined in this section: Endure. Hang on. Do not give up, no matter how hard the way becomes. Set aside shallow apocalyptic ideas.

The key vision in our chapter from Revelation is of making the here-and-now new. The New Jerusalem is not somewhere we need to travel to. It comes to us.

Moreover, this New Jerusalem is very different from the old Jerusalem because in it there is no temple. Does this mean that the vision is somehow a denial of the worship, ritual, and theological bias of all that has gone before? No more temple, no more church? Far from it. The temple is absent because the entire city is a temple; there is nowhere that is not temple; no time that is not worship. The certain sacred place and time is now the only place and time there is. There is no nowhere. Everywhere is *ha-makom*.

The New Jerusalem is *all* sacred space and time. All who live there are living totally and completely and finally in the image and likeness of God; the purpose of Genesis 1 is realized. It is the omega of which Genesis 1 is the alpha. Everything is the way God wants it to be. All is once again "good, very good."

Summary

But is all so totally well? Who, after all will be living there? "Only those who are written in the Lamb's Book of Life" (Rev. 21:27).

Endure; hang on; persist no matter how hard the way, for all will be well…for "us." Can this be the final word? As long as there remains an "us" and a "them," can we truly proclaim that all have received all the "help-we-need" as per the Abrahamic promise?

We still need help.

But there is no more to read. Revelation closes the Bible. What now?

Now we must sift, assess, and reflect. To this we will turn in *Speak Up—Faith Talking! an invitation to biblical living* soon to appear. Some guidance about this new task will in the meantime be given as we now examine the tone of voice we hear in the Bible.

14

Looking Forward

Two Stories of Tone

Tone of voice can be all important. The following stories come from my own experience. They are in no way profound. Each is, however, illustrative of tone.

Peterhead

Years ago I ministered in the town of Peterhead, far up on the eastern Aberdeenshire coast of Scotland. Peterhead has a long history of sea faring—first with whaling, then herring, followed by whitefish, and at the time I was there, oil and gas. It has a harsh climate, and those who make their living on and from the sea have a harsh life. Some years back Peterhead had become the Scottish home and headquarters of a Christian group known as the Plymouth Brethren or just "The Brethren" for short. This conservative movement was founded in the nineteenth century and espouses a fundamentalist view of the Bible—a combination of Calvinism, Pietism, and Puritanism with an emphasis on the Second Coming of Christ. Its worship stresses the weekly Breaking of the Bread, and there is no organized ordained ministry.

The Brethren displayed a sectarian mindset from the beginning, splitting very quickly into two main groups—the Open Brethren and the Closed or Exclusive Brethren. Both Open and Closed Brethren had meeting houses in Peterhead. As a minister at one of the local parishes of the Church of Scotland (a Presbyterian church) I had very little contact with them. We all seemed to live in two communities within the one town, the Brethren (both Open and Closed) on the one hand, and all other Christians on the other. We each had our own sheltered harbors from the harsh life around us.

I routinely walked the short half-mile or so from my house to my church, passing on the left-hand side an Open meeting house. I could not help but read their notice board. It indicated the times of services and added, "Everyone Welcome."

One Sunday evening I was walking home just after six and noticed that their evening service had just begun. I recalled a story told by my predecessor in that parish.

Walking home one evening as I was, and recalling that everyone was welcome he decided to go in and worship with them. He sat down quietly, and a hush fell over the room. The elder who had been speaking, preaching I suppose, drew in his breath, and pointing directly at him cried out, "There. There is the whore of Babylon. There."

He left them alone. He had unintentionally changed the tone in that small room. What had it become? It had become what, I fear, was always lingering, just beneath the surface.

Dumbarton

Some years later I was ministering in Dumbarton, a small Scottish city just outside of Glasgow and not far from the shores of Loch Lomond. Dumbarton had a proud history of shipbuilding (it was the site of Cutty Sark's construction, Cutty Sark being one of the greatest of all the great clippers), but by this time it was devoted to the whisky trade, both the manufacture and consumption thereof.

Our next-door neighbor was the local Baptist minister. One day he spoke to me about a "revival week" planned at his church. There was to be a guest preacher, an African-American whose name I have long since forgotten. The minister urged me to attend one of the planned evening services.

Towards the end of the week (I think it was Thursday) I made some time and headed off to his church. It was a great service, with tremendous singing in the Moody and Sankey revivalist tradition, and long but enthusiastic prayers. Then came the preacher who stirred the congregation and closed with "the invitation."

Altar calls are not part of the somewhat reserved Presbyterian liturgical tradition with which I was familiar, but I sat, watched, and waited to see "how it all worked." The organist slowly played verse after verse of "Just as I Am" familiar to me from TV productions of Billy Graham rallies. Between verses, the preacher exhorted and encouraged, reminding us of the key points of his sermon. After a few such verses it seemed to me that the preacher was almost begging. "Come forward and take Jesus into your heart; accept him as your personal Lord and Savior. Now, this very night, is your chance. Come forward." Nobody moved—until a man, whom I shall call Hugh, stood up.

I knew Hugh. He was a deacon in that Baptist church, aged about sixty, whose adult son was also a deacon. I had played golf with Hugh and his son from time to time. We had kidded each other about this and that aspect of church life, including our different traditions on baptism. Hugh was a pillar of the Baptist community in Dumbarton and one of that congregation's principal financial supporters. Hugh was the first, or should I say, the first finally to respond to the altar call. Others followed; Hugh after all was a leading deacon.

Hugh, of course, was helping out, trying to prime the pump, attempting to ease the preacher's agonized waiting. I watched in amazement as Hugh went forward to "receive Jesus as his Lord and Savior." He knelt and the preacher prayed with him, and then a couple of counselors came forward to usher Hugh out to a back room for "further instruction and to receive some literature."

I cannot recall how many (there weren't many) were spurred on by Hugh's example. The rest of the evening's worship is a bit of a haze in my memory. I was dumbfounded. The entire tone of the service had changed. Authenticity had been replaced by a well-intentioned charade.

Tones and Voices

In the preceding pages we have endeavored to hear eleven voices: history, torah, ritual, power, wisdom, prophecy, apocalyptic, encounter, escape, and endurance—each of which is an answer to the fundamental questioning voice of the Bible: We need help. How do we get it?

This question arose out of an archetypal recitation of the five great existential agonies of human life, discovered in our examination of Genesis 1–11: (1) What makes life good? (2) What makes life hard? (3) What makes life bad? (4) How is life possible? and (5) Can life be good again?

The foundational principle upon which we expected to find the "help-we-need" was articulated in the story of the call and promise to Abraham, namely that God loves and cares for the world. This love prompts the Abrahamic enterprise which in essence is a saving maneuver by God so that all peoples can realize their created purpose, to live in the image and likeness of God, to be God in and for one another and all creation.

The content of this foundational principle is love. The love of God for all peoples is its essential note.

Did all the voices we have noted speak with a loving tone or, at the least were they all dominated by such a tone? Is this tone the only tone we hear in the Bible?

Vengeful Anger, Smug Self-Satisfaction, and Pious Indifference

Psalm 137

The sixth-century BCE Babylonian Exile, as we have seen, was a devastating event in Israel's life. The glories and hopes of the treasured past had been shattered by the Babylonian military. In humiliation the people of Israel found themselves far from home. They were faced with a range of difficulties and challenges: how to make a living; how to adapt to a new culture and environment; how to retain a sense of pride and dignity; how to communicate to their children and young people their faith in the Abrahamic God who had been exalted in the Davidism doctrine of an imperishable Jerusalem; how to worship without the temple and its mandated sacrificial system; how to advocate the God of Moses in the midst of a culture ruled by Marduk, the Babylonian deity.

The astonishing power of Israel to survive manifested itself, not for the first or the last time in history. Priests, scholars, and scribes went about collecting the old traditions, written and oral, and put them together to become what we now know as the Torah. They also redacted the sayings of the great spokesmen of their God, who had warned and cajoled, encouraged and castigated them in the immediately preceding three hundred years or so. Thus, the second great volume of Scriptures came into being, the *Ketuvim*, the Prophets.

A new institution appeared, the synagogue, and there began the development of what would come to be known as the rabbinate.

And the people remembered. They told stories and sang songs of their past—extolling the wonders of their God and the glories of the lost Jerusalem.

Psalm 137 is one such song. Nostalgic, achingly mournful and full of longing, its tone is one of love for God and the glory of his city and temple. There is nothing wrong with its tone, and then it suddenly and radically changes. In verses 7–9 a harsh vindictiveness against Babylon rings out: "Happy the one who takes and dashes your little ones against the rock."

This tone is understandable, of course, at a purely human level. These people were captives, after all. Anger and a desire for revenge could not have been far below the surface of their strained psyches. Our problem, however, is how to hear these verses as part of the Word of God, for that is what the Bible is claimed to be by believers. *Does God speak in the tone of humanity's hateful rage?*

According to the Bible it seems that he does. Countless passages echo this tone.

Joshua 8

As we saw when we examined the Saul story, the practice of the *cherem* was an ancient military practice. *Cherem* means "ban" and what it entailed was the slaughter of all living things in a captured village, town, or city, as an offering, or tribute, to God. Several times in the Bible we read of God's commanding Israel's armies to enforce the *cherem*. The battle of Ai in our passage illustrates the *cherem's* consequences. "All" the inhabitants of Ai are slaughtered, not just the combatants. Note especially Joshua 8:26.

This issue here is not to evaluate ancient warfare techniques as if collateral damage were at all times avoided by "more civilized" armies. Collateral damage is precisely the objective of the *cherem,* just as it has been in more recent struggles (for example in the siege of Leningrad, the bombings of Dresden and Hiroshima, or the 9/11 attack on New York City's World Trade Center). The point for us is rather to catch the tone of Joshua 8. It is triumphal, exultant, and nationalistic.

Obadiah and Nahum

These two little prophetic books contain nothing but this tone. Obadiah in its entirety is a hateful and vindictive rant against Edom, issuing, of course, from the mouth and mind of God. (Remember who King Herod the Great was? An Idumean—a descendant of these Edomites.) Nahum does the same with Nineveh, the capital city of the despised Assyrians. Both these books represent a tendency and tone we can find in the pages of many of the prophets, who are also generally hailed as the champions, if not the inventors, of what is coyly called, "ethical monotheism." (See, for example, Isaiah 13–23 and Jeremiah 46–51.)

But this prophetic tone is directed not just at Israel's neighbors and enemies. Sometimes it falls on God's people themselves, as in Jeremiah 1–24 and in the book of Amos.

Acts 4:32–5:11

Not often does this tale feature on the Sunday morning preaching schedule. Nor could it be used in a class teaching caring pastoral techniques. Let's baldly recite and note carefully what happens.

- Ananias and Sapphira seek to cheat by withholding some of their wealth from the church, which had adopted a policy of holding all wealth in common.

- Ananias on his own brings in a portion of the money and offers it to the church, placing it at the feet of Peter.

- Peter somehow perceives that Ananias is cheating, tells him so, and emphasizes that in fact he is cheating not just the church but God.

- Hearing this Ananias collapses, dies, and his body is carried away.

- Some time later, unaware of what had happened to her husband, Sapphira enters, and Peter chooses to toy with her. Rather than compassionately telling her about her husband and that he, Peter, knows of the attempted cheat, he asks a few questions in such a way that she, too, lies and becomes party to the cheat.

- At that instant, Peter (pillar of the church after all) thunders in judgment, and she too instantly dies.

Running through the account of this incident is a certain smugness. The "great fear" of those witnessing it is repeatedly noted. I think the proverbial "fear of the Lord" may be intended but if so the passage terribly misconstrues what Proverbs means in 1:7 and 9:10. Far from the disturbed and self-preserving terror (of Peter, I think) suggested here in Acts, Proverbs extols a reverential awe towards God.

There is little to commend the tone, let alone the content, of this passage. It is petty, narrow-minded, self-righteous, and cruel. Where is the gospel promise of getting another chance, as exemplified in John 8:1–11? It is missing entirely.

John 3:1–21

So powerful and indelible in the Christian conscious is John 3:16 that it may be hard for me to make the case that it is but a part, a small part at that, of a passage that rings with smug indifference. Such, however, is the tone of this passage, if not of the entire gospel of John.

One of the recurring themes of John's gospel is that Jesus causes division amongst those who hear and witness his actions. John uses the Greek word *schisma* for this sense of divisiveness. So careful are we today to extol the virtues of unity, both in the church and in the world, it is hard to hear what John is actually saying. The consequence of Jesus coming "into the world" is its division into those who "believe in him" and those who do not. Those who do will "have eternal life" while those who do not "will perish."

In the companion volume to this book, *Speak Up—Faith Talking! an invitation to biblical living*, we shall have to deal with this. For now, I want to catch John's tone of voice. John is thought to refer to himself more than once in his gospel as "the disciple Jesus loved." Whatever else this may mean it indicates at the very least that he, John, thought that he was not to be numbered amongst those who would perish.

With that in mind reread our passage. How does it strike you? Nicodemus, believed by many scholars to be a member of the Jewish Sanhedrin, risks a lot by coming to Jesus at all, even "by night." It seems his inquiry is thoughtful and honest. Jesus takes it as such. What happens to his seeking and searching spirit? What happens to Nicodemus? Who knows? He is lost amidst a sea of red ink—John has Jesus talking and talking. Nicodemus simply disappears, fades away back into the night and the passage ends with the round and satisfied warnings of division to come.

The tone in this passage displays very little committed interest in others, at least in Nicodemus. (Please note very carefully that I am attributing this tone, *not to Jesus*, but to the author of John's gospel, a voice of the early church.) How does this square with the fundamental premise of the Abrahamic promise, that God loves the world? (You may be asking whether I am claiming that God loves at all costs, without any moral discernment. Be patient. We shall take up these issues in the companion volume. For now I am only trying to catch a biblical flavor.)

But there is another tone of voice in the Bible.

Long-Suffering Love

Hosea

In the Old Testament there is a Hebrew word that is so central and so hard to translate it ought really to become part of our English biblical vocabulary. It is the word *chesed*. (The accurate way to pronounce the first "ch" is as in Scottish "loch," or German "auch," but many find this sound difficult. A "k" sound will suffice.) This word is variously translated as "covenant love," "steadfast love," "patient love," "kindness," "mercy," to highlight the main options. It is a rich and dynamic term, indicating an attitude of total commitment and enduring patience.

Chesed is the love of God, and it is the love God is. It is the love at the foundation of the Abrahamic promise, and it is the voice we have been trying so desperately to hear through this book.

God is *chesed*. You may recall that I said grace was the adhering power of the love of God. Grace is actually God's love in action, applied. The great New Testament word for love is *agape*, in contrast to *eros* and *philia*. Each of these three words colors the Me/You relationship in terms of the how the needs of the other are met. (See Figure 23 in the appendix for an illustration of these dynamic interrelationships.)

Chesed teaches us that God's Abrahamic love is to meet our needs (to give us the "help-we-need") and that we in turn are to venture forth to meet the needs of the world (to be God in and for creation) so that "all" peoples will be blessed. To ensure that *chesed* does not remain a mere notion, some sort of distant ideal, grace is part of it; grace is *chesed*'s sticking power. Not only does this mean that we cannot shake off God's love, but it also means that we in turn must go on loving all peoples.

Chesed is *agape* plus grace. It is the notion of God's love plus its inevitable sticking power. *Chesed* is true love.

The prophecy of Hosea is all about such love. (How strange that there are Christians who think that the "discovery" that God is love and that he can be addressed as "father" are peculiarly Christian treasures. The distinctiveness of Christianity lies elsewhere.)

The story (of which Hosea's prophecies are the reflected meaning) is simply told. His wife Gomer was a prostitute either at the time of their marriage or some time thereafter. By law Hosea had the right, even the duty, to divorce her. Hosea chooses instead a life of *chesed*...a life of long-suffering, patient, redemptive love. By extension, the prophet applies this to God and his relationship to his faithless bride, Israel.

The tone matches the content. Hosea announces God's displeasure with Israel's unfaithfulness (her going after other gods in a syncretistic frenzy) but he always returns to a longing summons, almost, one might say, a soft wooing of the people, urging them to return.

This is the tone of the restorative power of *chesed*.

Pre-Abrahamic Chesed

We have encountered *chesed* before: in the stories of Adam and Eve not receiving their due punishment and of God making clothes for them; of Cain, being marked for protection after hearing of his punishment; and perhaps supremely in the story of the Flood, sent to wipe out all life but sparing Noah and the others in the floating tomb that was the ark. It is *chesed* that lies behind the call of Abram and the rescuing ministry of Moses. *Chesed* is the heartbeat of Israel's history.

The *chesed* tone is a verbal form of the visual rainbow at the Flood's end.

Chesed is the attribute of God that makes him ever lean towards empowerment over eradication.

Jonah

Jesus told his contemporaries that the only sign available to them was the sign of Jonah. Perhaps, as many argue, he intended this to be a preparatory prediction of his Resurrection. Just as Jonah emerged from the whale's belly after three days so too would Jesus emerge from the grave. Perhaps this is what he intended, but I do not think so.[67]

The story of Jonah is precisely a story of the collision of the two tones of voice we have isolated. It can be easily outlined:

- Jonah is summoned by God to journey east to Nineveh, the hated capital city of Israel's Assyrian enemies, to preach a message of God's love for them and call them to repentance.

- Jonah immediately heads off west across the sea in the opposite direction. He wants no part of this tone of voice or its content.

- A storm leads him to offer himself to the crew as a sacrifice (he knew that he had been disobedient) and into the sea he is thrown. He ends up in the belly of a whale.

- The whale vomits him onto dry land, and he reluctantly proceeds east to Nineveh.

- On his arrival he proclaims, in a cursory and abbreviated manner, God's message of love and his summons to repentance.

- Lo and behold, it works. The Assyrians repent.

- Jonah furiously blames God, "See; I told you so. I told you these people whom I hate and whom you should too, would repent if I proclaimed your word to them. I told you."

- Jonah sits beneath a bush and sulks. How horrid it is that God loves people I hate.

The impatient, hateful, churlish, angry tone of Jonah's voice is drowned out by the tone of God's *chesed*. *Chesed* will fulfill its Abrahamic promise despite our all-too-human prejudices and preferences.

Surely that is the "only sign" we need.

A Choice

John Calvin taught that, when confused about a Scripture passage, we should always allow Scripture to correct Scripture. There are many other tones of voice in the Bible: disputatious, proud, arrogant, worried, fearful, joyful, prayerful, and sincere. The two we have focused on, however, are at polar opposites. Each echoes the great ethical option—eradication or empowerment. Each can be heard in the believing community today. They are not consistent one with another. Following Calvin's advice where are we led?

I believe we are led squarely to tune out the voice of vengeful anger, smug self-satisfaction, and pious indifference. On what basis do I make this assertion? I believe it is a tone so totally out of tune with the *chesed* voice of the Abrahamic promise that it drowns that voice out. The foundational premise of the Bible is *chesed*. Voices whose tones deny or contradict that are not to be listened to or at least are to be brought in tune, if possible, with this overriding sound.

There is no choice. To stand on the side of empowerment against eradication is the only biblical option. Biblical people must speak the language of *chesed*.

Chesed living is biblical living.
How to do this?

Epilogue
Two Voices

In this book we have heard eleven voices. The eleven can, in essence, be divided into two parts.

- The first is the questioning voice.

Based on the great archetypal stories of Genesis 1–11, this voice is one that cries out for help. In crying out it proclaims our need: We need help! We need help to live the life God intends for us—to care for all creation, to live always and everywhere in sacred space and time. And so humanity asks: Where is the help? How can we access it?

- The second part comprises the answering voices.

These remaining voices all offer answers to this fundamental need of the human spirit. They are: History, Torah, Ritual, Power, Wisdom, Prophecy, Apocalyptic, Encounter, Escape, and Endurance. Each voice offers help, but each offers less than the help we need. Each contains within itself some inadequacy, even if that inadequacy is nothing more than our own inability to accept or respond to the answer's demand. There must be more. The question and the answers that follow cannot be all that the Bible has to say to us, can they?

A Third Voice

The bottom-line assertion of this book is that the help-we-need can be found when we live a life of *chesed*—demonstrating God's steadfast love—in the world. How are we to do that? What do we need to know?

The answers to these questions can be found in

a. the rest of the Bible,

b. the entire body of theology that followed it,

c. and the mission and work of the church.

Think about it. *The rest of the Bible, every syllable of theology, every action and activity of the church—all of these things are supposed to show us how to live the life of* chesed. *Any part of these three that does not meet that purpose is superfluous and pretentious.* The explaining voice of faith must be a servant of the questioning and answering voices of the Bible, pure and simple.

So, finally, I can ask: Do we need help to live the life of *chesed* and, if so, how do we get that help? My next book, the companion volume to this one, will be called *Speak Up!—An Invitation to Biblical Living.* In it I hope to provide answers to these final questions.

APPENDIX

In the Preface I stated that a fault of most Sunday school curricula is their tendency to divide the Bible up into teachable quarter units in such a way as to render incomprehensible the Bible as a whole. These curricula are slaves to "snippetology" whereby the Bible is broken apart into three year cycles, rendering any comprehension of it as a whole extremely unlikely. In such curricula the various stories stand apart from one another and the Bible remains an odd and strange mystification. This is a tragedy, for what is missed are God's plan, his will, his chesed, and his power. A hidden aim of this book has been to bring the unified intent of the Bible to the reader's attention. The Bible, after all, is *a* book; it is *a* redaction, put together for *a* reason. It is about the *chesed* adventure, which leads to *chesed* living, the challenges of which the companion volume to this book, *Speak Up—Faith Talking! an invitation to biblical living*, will attempt to make clear. We shall see there that becoming a *chesed* community requires institutional integrity and personal courage.

I am convinced that the New Testament in general and the story of Jesus in particular remain opaque and subject to emotionalist and/or superstitious interpretation when divorced from a thorough grounding in the Old Testament. The ministry of the early church, as told in Acts and revealed in Paul's letters, flows naturally from the ministry of Jesus. His ministry, however, is frankly incomprehensible when torn out of its context. This context is greatly illumined by a grasp of the Hebrew Scriptures as a whole. This grasp is the key to true Christian education.

The maps, charts, idiot sentences, and illustrations which follow are intended as *aides memoires*, but in fact they offer far more than a teaching gimmick or technique. If these are understood *together* then a grasp of the Hebrew Scriptures will be attained which will far surpass that engendered by every Sunday school curriculum I know. The context for the ministry of Jesus, and thus for everything that followed will become clear.

A further outline of more material carrying the Christian education adventure on from the point where it is left here will appear in *Speak Up—Faith Talking! an invitation to biblical living.*

A two year Bible reading plan is also offered which is designed to make all this clear.

These *aides memoires* offer the skeleton for a bold new approach to Christian education curriculum building.

A) Diagrammatic Maps

Many excellent maps are found in various study Bibles and Bible Atlases. My experience with students, however, tells me that many people have trouble correctly reading maps and getting a true feel for the scope of what they illustrate. The diagrammatic maps which are presented in the appendix are meant to aid in the subsequent task of examining actual biblical maps in a good atlas.

1. Figure 1: The Ancient Middle East

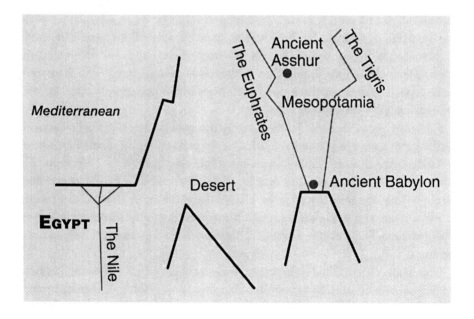

2. Figure 2: The Holy Land

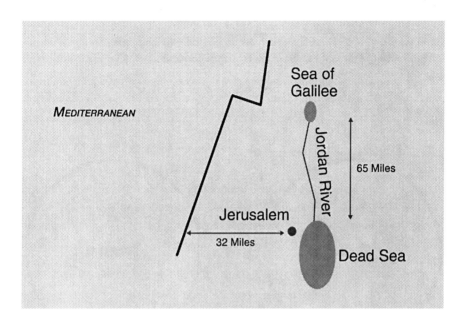

3. Figure 3: The Mediterranean Basin

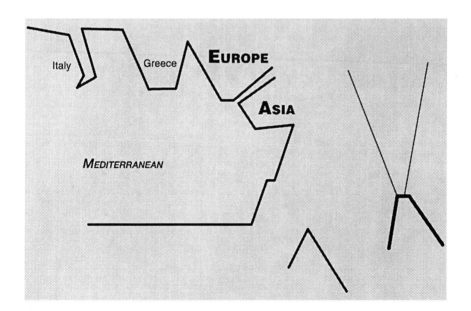

B) Figure 4: The Fundamental Assumption of the Bible

The Bible does not seek to prove the existence of God. It assumes (a) *there is God* and (b) *the world is not God*. This difference of God from the world, God's utter otherness from the world, is called transcendence. It can be illustrated as follows:

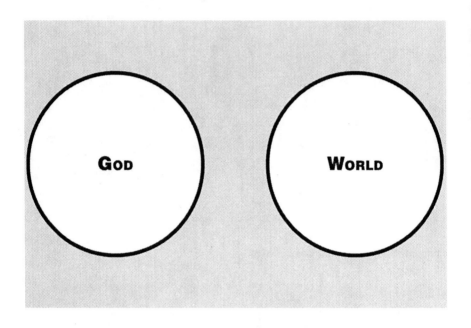

C) Figure 5: The Fundamental Premise of the Bible

If God is utterly other than the world, how can the world ever know anything about God? The Bible asserts that *God relates to the world*. This relating can be regarded as traces left behind in the creation of and by the creator (so-called natural or general revelation) or as indications given in and through special people, events, and places (so-called special revelation.) This can be illustrated as follows:

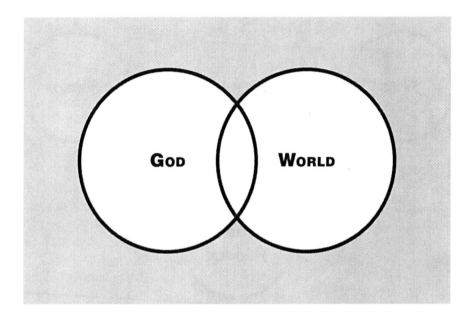

D) Figure 6: The Fundamental Dynamic of the Bible

God seeks to give the world the help it needs to become all that he wishes it to be (good, very good.) He does this through selecting a people to bring his will and word to the world so that the world can return close to him (the Abrahamic promise, the empowerment over eradication option, the incarnation principle, etc.)

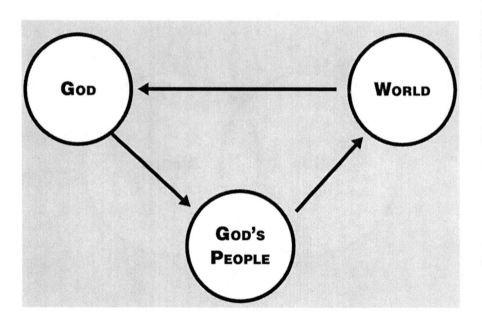

E) The Six Idiot Sentences

In the sentences which follow the first letter is the key letter. Together these six sentences provide a chronological and theologically sequential structure of the Hebrew Scriptures major people and the events in which they were involved and caught up.

One: The major foreign peoples

Can **E**ager **A**llan [**S**impson] **B**ring **P**atricia **G**orgeous **R**oses

Canaanites Egyptians Assyrians [Samaritans] Babylonians Persians Greeks Romans
2000   800   587   333   63......

Two: Major OT Figures One
An Insane Jolly Jumping Man Just Slew Slippery Spaghetti Down Stairs
Abraham Isaac Jacob Joseph Moses Joshua Samson Samuel Saul David Solomon
2000   1500–1300   1000   900

Three: Major Events One
Come Play With Susan Except When Carol Cummings Kisses Stephen
Call/Promise Wandering Slavery Exodus Wilderness Covenant Conquest Kingdom Split
2000   1500–1300   1000   900

Four: Major OT Figures Two
Every Elephant In Jamaica Eats [Delicious] Hot Zebras Each Night
Elijah Elisha Isaiah Jeremiah Ezekiel [Daniel] Haggai Zechariah Ezra Nehemiah
900   750   650   580   500   400

Five: Major Events Two
Dumb   Fred   Eats   Raw   Ham
Decay   Fall   Exile   Recovery   Hope
900   597–97   500   167............

Six: Intertestamental Keys
Andy   Held   Maggie   Romantically
Alexander   Hellenization   Maccabees Romans
333   167   165   63

F) Patterns of Geschichte

   In the following diagrams the zero or starting point is the call and promise to
Abram. With this begins the coming of the help-we-need which embodies *chesed*
as the reality of God's will as empowerment not eradication. Thus, biblical history is not a shallow attempt to recount what actually happened (*Historie*) but
rather a serious attempt to show the meaning of what happened (*Geschichte.*)
Each of the diagrams below offers illustrations of the Idiot Sentences Two
through Six above in the same order. These sentences placed on the value-added
timeline illustrate the dynamic of the biblical witness.

Figure 7: *Idiot Sentence Two as Geschichte*

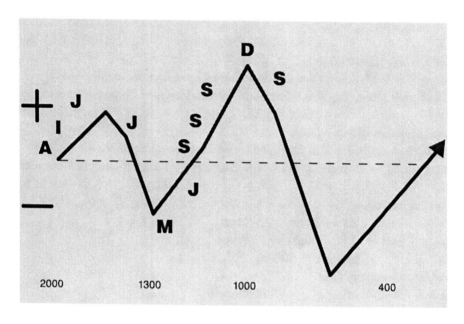

Figure 8: *Idiot Sentence Three as Geschichte*

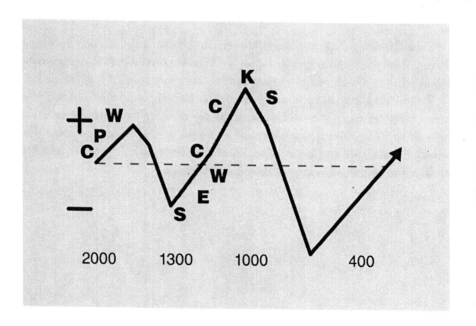

Figure 9: *Idiot Sentence Four as Geschichte*

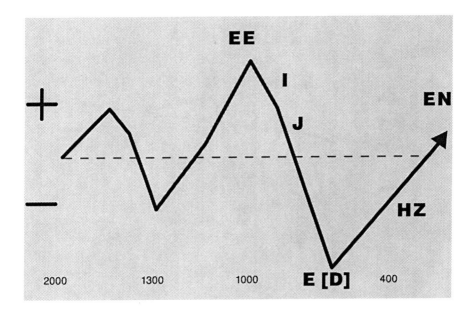

Figure 10: *Idiot Sentence Five as Geschichte*

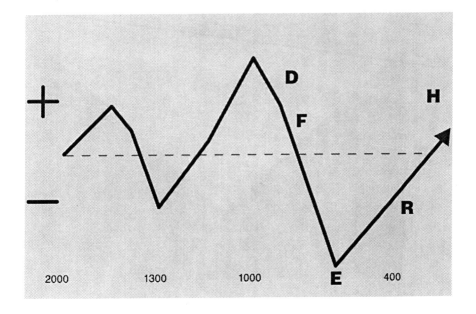

Figure 11: *Idiot Sentence Six as Geschichte*

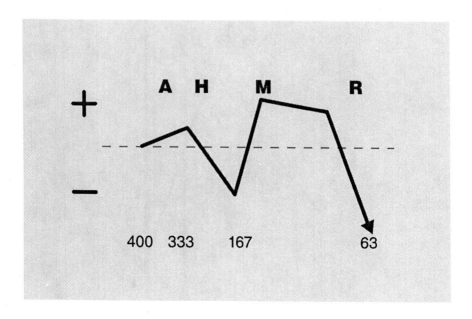

G) Figure 12: The Archetypal Process

H) Figure 13: First Century Factions

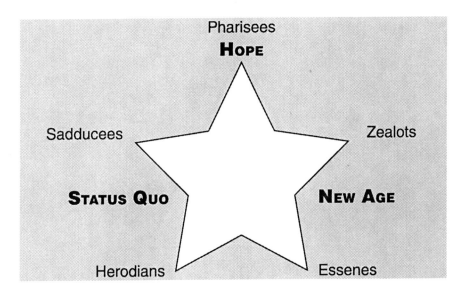

I) The Shapes of the Answering Voices
Figure 14: Torah: covering all aspects of life all the time

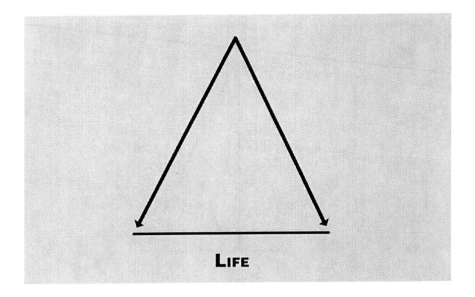

Figure 15: Ritual: creating a certain place of sacred space and time

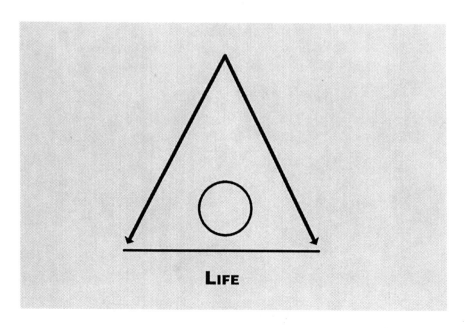

Figure 16: Power: seizing control of the ups and downs of history

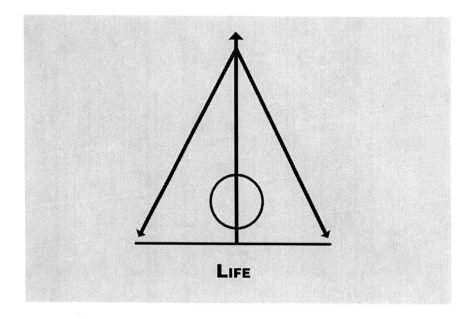

Figure 17: Wisdom: encircling life in a cover of usefulness and reliability

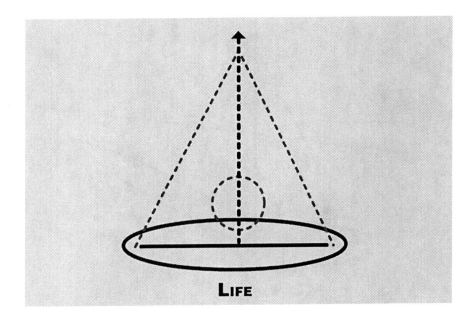

Figure 18: Prophecy: sweeping life forward with ethical urgency

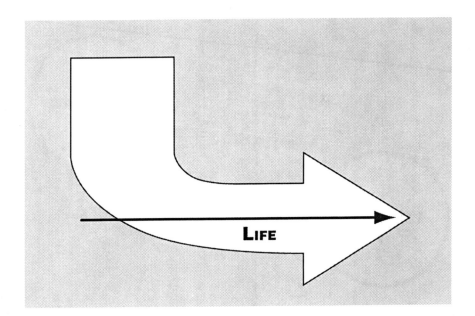

Figure 19: Apocalyptic: carrying life away to another realm and time

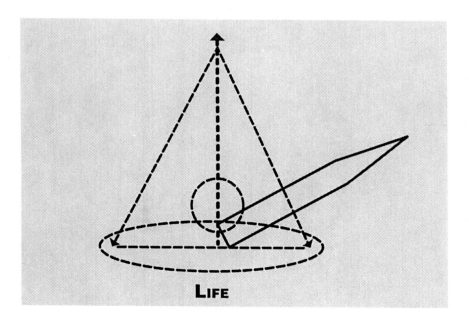

Figure 20: Escape: a Christianized view of apocalyptic

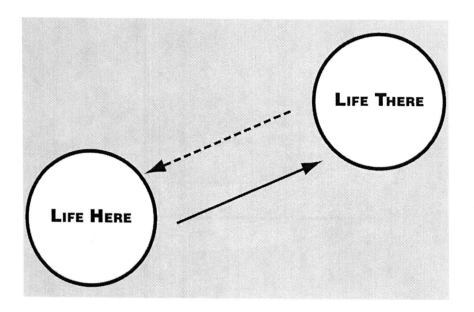

Figure 21: Endurance: a Christianized view of

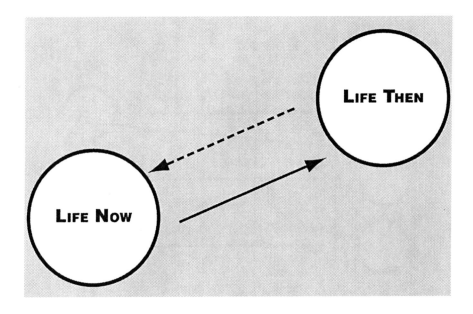

J) Figure 22: The Structure of the Temple

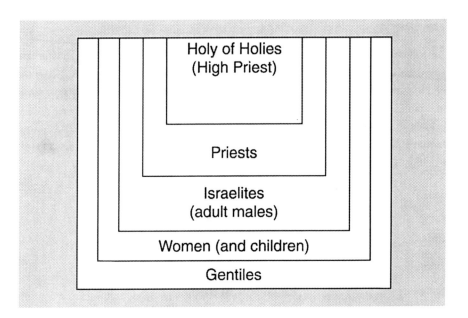

K) Figure 23: The Dynamic of Love

L) Bible Reading Plan

Year One

The following list provides 363 chapters of the Bible. If you omit Easter and Christmas days, you have a year's plan of one chapter per day. You can begin any time, any day. Begin now. Never skip a day. Even on your busiest day you surely can spare 7-10 minutes to read a single chapter.

These chapters have been explicitly selected to make clear the reality of God's covenant plan of salvation, of the triumph of grace over sin. The chapters must be read in the order listed below.

Genesis	50 chapters
Exodus	40 chapters
Joshua	24 chapters
Judges	21 chapters
1 Samuel	31 chapters

2 Samuel	24 chapters
1 Kings	22 chapters
2 Kings	25 chapters
Isaiah 40-66	27 chapters
Malachi	4 chapters
Mark	16 chapters
1 John	5 chapters
James	5 chapters
Acts	28 chapters
Philippians	4 chapters
John	21 chapters
Romans	16 chapters

Year Two

The readings this year build on the knowledge of the Bible's scope, gained from Year One's reading plan. With the Old Testament readings, an effort is made to hear the urgency of the voice of the prophets' as they bring God's word to bear in various contexts. This pattern is balanced with interspersed readings from Book One of The Psalms. With the New Testament, two more gospels (Matthew and Luke) are read, together with two major, though very different, reflections on the significance of Jesus (Hebrews and Ephesians.) Additionally there are some documents dealing with problems and issues from the early church's growing period. As with Year One, this year's Reading Plan offers 363 chapters, one per day with Christmas and Easter as rest days. The chapters must be read in the order listed below.

Old Testament

Prophecy Spoken in Israel, the northern Kingdom, as the Assyrian Threat Mounted in the 8th century

Amos	9 chapters
Hosea	14 chapters
and Psalms 1-6	6 chapters

Prophecy spoken in Judah, the southern kingdom, during the 8th century crisis

Micah	7 chapters
Isaiah 1-39	39 chapters
and Psalms 7-12	6 chapters

Prophecy spoken in Judah as the Babylonian threat mounted in the 7th century

Jeremiah	52 chapters
and Psalms 13-18	6 chapters

Prophecy spoken as the Babylonian threat led to actual exile in Babylon, into the 6th century

Ezekiel	48 chapters
and Psalms 19-24	6 chapters

History of the Period of the Return from Exile, 5th century

Nehemiah	13 chapters
Ezra	10 chapters
and Psalms 25-30	6 chapters

Prophecy of the Period of the Return, 5th century

Haggai	2 chapters
Zechariah 1-8	8 chapters
and Psalms 31-36	6 chapters

Prophecy of the Period following the Greek Conquest

Zechariah 9-14	5 chapters
Daniel	12 chapters
and Psalms 37-41	5 chapters

New Testament

Matthew	28 chapters
Hebrews	13 chapters
Luke	24 chapters
Ephesians	6 chapters
1 Corinthians	16 chapters
1 Thessalonians	5 chapters
Galatians	6 chapters
1 Peter	5 chapters

Endnotes

1. The outstanding work of *the Kerygma program* is designed to rectify this situation, but *Kerygma's* very existence points to the presence of the problem. See *the Kerygma program*, 300 Mt. Lebanon Blvd., Pittsburgh, PA 15234, or at www.kerygma.com.

2. I use this description firmly hoping that there is no actual Professor Gumpelheimer. If there is an actual Professor Gumpelheimer, I apologize. I am sure he/she is doing a super job.

3. See note 6 below for advice on which translation to use. If at all possible an edition with no study guide material at all would be best for the purposes of this book.

4. The idea that Christianity, its books, and its theology renders the Hebrew Scriptures with any Jewish interpretations of them or other Jewish voices of witness to their truth somehow irrelevant to a Christian understanding is called "supersessionism." Christianity is thought to supersede Jewish contributions and insights. It is a form of ideological imperialism. This and other Jewish-Christian ideas are discussed expertly in the volume <u>Christianity in Jewish Terms</u>, edited by Tikva Frymer-Kensky et al, Westview Press, Boulder, 2000. I thoroughly reject supersessionism as even a remotely adequate option for Christian theology.

5. Throughout this book I will use BCE (before the common era) and CE (common era) rather than the BC (Before Christ) and AD (*anno domini*, Year of the Lord) designations.

6. There has been a virtual explosion of "new translations" of the Bible since the middle of the twentieth century. The King James Version, so dominant in Protestant churches for so many generations, has grown nearly silent. Amongst the many more recent translations

Today's English Version [the so-called Good News Bible] is the clearest example of the philosophy of needing to find contemporary target language expressions for source language archaisms. Its popularity has waned in recent decades. Every translation is, to some extent a paraphrase, but some are explicitly paraphrases, not working with the source languages at all. They should be read accordingly. It is as well to note that we all are meant to be bilingual, fluent in the language of the street, which we speak, and the language of the essay, which we write. Of the many translations available the two which perhaps most nearly approximate the way contemporary Americans think and are supposed to write English are the New International Version and the New American Standard Bible.

7. The Bible's patriarchalism is perhaps the clearest of these realities. It must be recognized for what it is; a cultural tendency shared by many other cultures of a day now gone by. Many of the ancient Greek archetypal stories of conflict between goddesses and gods reflect what was in fact an historical collision between ancient patriarchal societies and their even more ancient matriarchal competitors. As far as the Bible is concerned its patriarchalism, as seen in its acceptance of polygamy for example, must not be translated into terms of the contemporary debate concerning female rights. The cultural pressures, for example brought on by the perilous nature of child-birth at the time, were very distinct from our cultural pressures. Equally, of course, the Bible's patriarchalism cannot in any sense be interpreted as "revealed truth" establishing itself as God's will for the male-female relationship for all time.

8. See, for example, Michael Drosnin, The Bible Code, Touchstone, NY, 1998.

9. Having written these words I came across the same idea being used to illustrate another, very different point, in Marcus J. Borg, The Heart of Christianity: rediscovering a life of faith, Harper, San Francisco, 2003, pp. 221-22.

10. The plural here should not be thought to indicate that it is to be translated "gods." It is a grammatical plural indicating intensity, not number. The verb accompanying it is *bara*, the Hebrew verb for the third person singular, "he created." The later phrase where God is reported to have said, "Let us" in no way can be used to support a plural translation of *elohim* either; it is a usage not unlike the "royal we." Some scholars have argued that elohim refers to a heavenly council, like the Creator's Cabinet if you will, a concept familiar from other ancient religions. Perhaps this may be an echo, but again the singular *bara* belies this. Christian theologians who see in *elohim* some reference to the Trinity such that God the Father can later be thought in the "Let us" to be having a chat with the pre-existent Son of God are guilty of a trend we shall be speaking of in Speak Up—Faith Talking! an invitation to biblical living, namely reading the Bible backwards.

11. The dominion spoken of here is often said to be the cause for that hubris which has led humanity, more and more as the generations have passed and civilization become more sophisticated, to exploit and "lord it over" Nature as though the world were there for humanity's amusement and existed solely as a resource for human existence. Dominion, it is true, does derive from the Latin *dominus*, meaning Lord. This passage does indeed give humanity dominion and thus humans are to be Lord in the world. The point, however, is that this lordship is in the image of God and thus the dominion is one of caring not mastery. The rape of the planet cannot be attributed to the role given humanity in Genesis. God the Creator is not to blame for human stupidity and selfishness. More on human freedom later in this book.

12. See Dan Brown, The DaVinci Code, Doubleday, New York, 2003. This book is wondrously ill-informed and outright dishonest in many of its claims. We read on p. 309: "Langdon's Jewish students always looked flabbergasted when he first told them that the early Jewish tradition involved ritualistic sex. In the Temple no less. Early Jews believed that the Holy of Holies in Solomon's Temple housed

not only God but also His powerful female equal, Shekinah. Men seeking spiritual wholeness came to the Temple to visit priest-esses—or hierodules—with whom they made love and experienced the divine through physical union. The Jewish tetragrammaton YHWH—the sacred name of God—in fact derived from Jehovah, an androgynous physical union between the masculine Jah and the pre-Hebraic name for Eve, Havah." Where to start??? There is so much wrong with this. First, the hieros gamos or sacred marriage ritual was a prominent part of Canaanite as well as Mesopotamian and Egyptian cultic practice. Hierodules, or female cultic slaves, were a part of almost every known goddess cult in ancient times. The absence of ritualistic sex in ancient Israel was one of its most remarkable points. No wonder "Langdon's Jewish students always looked flabbergasted." There is no evidence whatsoever that such cultic practices ever took place in the Temple. The word "shekinah" is not in the Old Testament. It derives from the Hebrew verb *sha-kan*, to settle down, to dwell, which lies behind the word *mishkan* meaning dwelling-place or tabernacle. Shekinah as such does not occur and it was not until the Kabalistic literature many centuries later that it evolved its full-blown female overtones. The word was used by non-kabalistic Jews, however, to denote God's visible pres-ence. As for Shekinah somehow being a female equal of God, this is a mistake I suppose based on the fact that it is a feminine noun lin-guistically speaking. A feminine noun need not point to a female entity. Linguistic gender has nothing to do with sexual reality. For example Das Frau is a neuter noun in German but it means "the wife".... As for YHWH, here is what we need to know (we will return to this important matter later.) It was only in the Middle Ages that the rabbis permitted vowels to be added to the text of the Hebrew Bible. Prior to that, only consonants were written, as in modern Hebrew today—and the context helped to explain the meaning. Sometimes the scribes would add a word in the margin of the text to help the reader. This margin word is referred to as the "Qere" [what is to be read out loud] as distinct from the "Ketib" [what is written.] When they came to YHWH, the name for God, they always inserted a Qere, because nobody was meant to pronounce the Ketib of this most holy word. In fact, over the centuries they forgot what the word was to sound like altogether. Anyhow, the most common Qere for YHWH was the word Adonai, which means "my Lord." In the middle Ages, when the rabbis were finally persuaded to add vowels to the text, they inserted the Qere vowels of Adonai to the Ketib consonants YHWH, understanding that the Qere was still what was to be read out loud. When the translators created the King James Bible they found the following in the Hebrew manuscripts: YeHoWaH, and wrongly thought it said "JeHoVaH." Jehovah is not a Hebrew word at all; it is gobbledygook. The one certainty about the name of God is that it is not Jehovah. Today some modern English translations use "Yahweh" but most translate the Hebrew word YHWH as LORD—with a capital "L" and small capitals for the rest. The pre-Hebraic name for Eve???? Genesis itself derives her name from "havah"—pronounced sort of like Eva—and is the Hebrew word for "living" or "life." There is nothing pre-Hebrew about it. Fiction again.

13. The fruit was almost certainly not an apple, as apple trees were not native to the area of the Genesis authors. The reference to "fig leaves" which immediately follows their becoming aware of their nakedness suggests that the tree of the knowledge of good and evil was a fig tree.

14. See R. G. Collingwood, The Idea of History, revised edition, Oxford University Press, Oxford, 1994.

15. The Bible begins by assuming that there is God and that the world is not God (as illustrated in the appendix, Figure 4). The horror the Bible expresses at idolatry stems from this for idolatry in essence is taking the world or some part of it as God in and for your life. Indeed the voice of "the devil" can be understood as the lure of the world or some part of it insinuating itself as God for you.

16. The earliest form the church's understanding of the Cross took was to see in it *Christus Victor*, that is Christ as victor over the devil and all his forces. The Christ event was supremely a winning of the battle we are alluding to. See the classic <u>Christus Victor</u>, by Gustaf Aulen, SPCK, London, 1931.

17. "You cannot serve God and mammon," Matthew 6:24 and Luke 16:13.

18. In the New Testament following the death/suicide of Judas and convinced that the number twelve is important, the remaining eleven apostles decide to add one more to their number. They do not survey resumes, but select two and then throw dice to decide which one has been pre-selected by God. This story is told in Acts 1: 15-26.

19. Note that the correct reference is not to "the God of Abraham, Isaac, and Jacob." The phrase "the God of" precedes each name thereby indicating that each generation must absorb and adopt the reality of being God's people. As is commonly said, God has no grandchildren.

20. In many archetypal stories from the ancient world the revealing of a god or goddess to a human resulted in the human's death. Such a sight, such knowledge, of the divine totality was regarded as beyond human comprehension. There are many such examples, but one is the story from Greek archetypal mythology of Zeus being seen in all his divinity by Semele, who is instantly consumed in flames. In the Hebrew Scriptures this idea finds expression in a later story of Moses and God when God, in response to Moses' pleading to see him face to face, offers him instead a glimpse of his back. Theology retains this idea in its understanding of the dynamic of revelation, contained in the Latin saying, *Deus revelatus Deus velatus*, God revealed is God veiled. Luther spoke of this in his notion of the *deus absconditus*, that the God of revelation reveals only part of his reality and that there remains the hidden God. See Figure 5 in the appendix.

21. This dimension of the revealed name is retained in Judaism through its reluctance to pronounce the name. The current glib tendency in Christian circles to allow the name "Yahweh" to spill onto the page and out of the mouth thoroughly ignores or abandons this cautionary tone. Never use this name for God.

22. This was the inspired insight of Buber and Rozenzweig in their translation of the Hebrew Scriptures, recently reissued, <u>Die Schrift</u>, Gätersloher Verlagshaus, 1997.

23. Scholars have identified two separate traditions of the succession story. In the one Saul meets David as a harp-playing shepherd, invited to come to soothe the troubled spirit of the king–David as therapist, if you will. In the other, they first meet one another just prior to the battle with Goliath–David as warrior. Thus, we see at work the continuing reality of redaction and the decision not to obliterate one side of the tradition in favor of the other, but to include both. By the way, David as therapist to the troubled and David as warrior for the threatened are highly suggestive of two different modes of understanding the role of the church in the world.

24. This opposition of Law and Gospel depends on a narrow reading of Law in terms of guilt and punishment. This, as we shall see, is not the whole of what the Gospel must say about the relationship of humanity before God.

25. There are several covenants in the Scripture: between God and Noah; Abraham; Moses; David; the individual heart as in Jeremiah, and Jesus. An important issue in Christian theology is whether these covenants displace or complement one another. Some Christian theologians maintain that the covenant with Jesus supplants all the preceding covenants, a view sometimes dubbed "supersessionism." This is a view I thoroughly reject. See note 4 above.

26. The priority of God's grace is a key to understanding the power of the "help-we-need." It accounts for the Christian practice of infant baptism which enacts the great before of God: before we know him;

he knows us: before we come to love him or choose him, he has promised us his love and already has chosen us.

27. In world religions there are three forms of theism. Polytheism derives from the Greek *poly* meaning "many" gods or goddesses. Various divine beings are called upon at different stages and in different aspects of life. A man, for example, may pray to the god of harvest if he is a farmer and yet, when called upon to fight in battle, may call upon the god of war, only later, on his return home, to call on the goddess of fertility as he and his wife seek to have a child. Henotheism derives from the Greek for "one." Properly henotheism is the form of theism which relates to *one amongst many* divine beings. It does not deny or compete with polytheism, but simply asserts that only one god/goddess is to be related to at every stage and in all aspects of a life. Monotheism derives from the Greek for "single, only." Monotheism involves the assertion that other gods/goddesses are not real in any sense apart from or distinct from the only theos. Some scholars argue that behind its apparent polytheism Hinduism with its notion of brahman is in fact monotheistic. Determining a given religion's theism is by no means an easy task. With the call to tolerance so widespread today in the church, for example, is it not the case that many Christians could be regarded as henotheistic?

28. Matthew, Mark, and Luke each recount this incident in slightly different ways. The Sh'ma, Judaism's confession of faith, includes Deuteronomy 6: 4 which refers to loving God, "with all your heart, and with all your soul, and with all your might." In both Mark and Luke a fourth element is introduced, "with all your mind." It seems to me unlikely that a Jew would add to the confession this way. All three incidents add Leviticus 19:18 with the injunction to love neighbor as self.

29. This is part of what lies behind the story of Mary and Joseph offering two doves following the birth of Jesus, Luke 2:22–27, although

Luke seems to confuse it with rites of purification of a mother following childbirth.

30. Sometimes it is argued that church or synagogue attendance is not necessary to worship God, that he can equally well be worshipped in the kitchen, at the office, on the golf course, and in the boat. This is true. However, the point is not if God *can* be worshipped in these places, each of which can be *Ha-makom*, but whether he *will* in fact be. I have heard God's name invoked many times on the golf course—seldom in worship.

31. Alvin Toffler, Future Shock, Bantam, 1984.

32. J. T. Fraser, Time: The Familiar Stranger, Tempus, 1987.

33. The others are: *shahadah*, the recitation of the confession, "There is no God but Allah and Muhammad is his messenger;" *zakat*, the giving of 2.5% of disposable income to charity; *saum*, observing the month long fast of Ramadam, and *hajj*, the obligation to make a pilgrimage to Mecca once in a lifetime.

34. See, for example, the several works on the subject by William McKane, who taught me while he was still at Glasgow University before moving on to St. Andrews.

35. This duality of the object of awe, its total otherness and its present lure, is captured magnificently by Rudolf Otto in his classic The Idea of the Holy, Oxford, 1924. Otto speaks of the Other as the *mysterium tremendum et fascinans*. The "*et fascinans*" articulates the lure aspect.

36. This is in such stark contrast to so much in contemporary culture and church, so driven by charisma, celebrity, and personality.

37. This effort was not unlike what would be witnessed to so many times in so many places in medieval Europe, where beautiful, huge cathedrals were often built amidst squalor and desperate need.

38. Jacob Neusner, one of the twentieth century's greatest Judaica scholars, frequently uses this term. See for example Introduction to

Rabbinic Literature, Doubleday, New York, 1994, for which it is the guiding premise. He had earlier used the phrase in his An Introduction to Judaism, Westminster/John Knox, Louisville, 1991, 157. Neusner also makes clear that his use of the word "Judaism" is meant to indicate what he calls "Judaisms."

39. To some extent this has continued in Judaism down to the present day. It is heard in the Passover refrain, "Next year in Jerusalem."

40. In recent times the same concern has found new expression; see Alan Dershowitz, The Vanishing American Jew: In Search of Jewish Identity for the Next Century, Touchstone, New York, NY, 1997

41. We shall take up the matter of dating of New Testament books and events below.

42. Philip Yancey, in The Bible Jesus Read, Zondervan, Grand Rapids, 1999, writes about Job, Ecclesiastes and Psalms, as well as a few others. None of these three works were regarded as "the Bible" in Jesus' day, although the Psalms through their familiar use in the worship of the Temple hovered on the edge of being regarded as of the same status as "the Law and the prophets." It is totally unclear if Jesus was even familiar with, let alone moved by, those other works which are now part of the Ketuvim.

43. Hanukah, from the Hebrew for "dedication," is the first non-biblical Jewish festival. Until the eighteenth century Haskalah (Jewish enlightenment) it was a minor celebration, but since that time it has taken on increasing significance amongst Jewish populations living in the midst of Christian Christmas celebrations which occur at the same time of year. In Israel today Hanukah has also taken on tones of celebrating Israeli military prowess and national rebirth. Hanukah is mainly celebrated in the Jewish home, although there are additional prayers prescribed for the synagogue liturgy. Most visible of the Hanukah practices is the lighting of the special hanukiyah, a candelabrum with nine candle holders. The usual menorah has only seven candles, but most Jews refer to the Hanukah candle-holder as a menorah anyway. Eight candles symbolize the eight days of the

festival while the ninth, the so-called *shamash* or servant, is used to light the others each night. The candles are to be placed in their holders from right to left and then lit from left to right and thus the last added is lit first. (The last shall be first.) The candles are to be placed in the home so that they can be seen from the outside. Certain blessings are recited along with the lighting. Hanukah also is a time for family fun, as in playing *dreidl*, the Yiddish for spinning top. The game is known as *s'vivon* in Hebrew. Latkes are traditionally eaten at Hanukkah, but thankfully are not restricted to this holiday.

44. For more on these dates as they apply to the birth of Jesus, see note 49.

45. Such a direct military confrontation finally did take place in the early decades of the second century CE. Interestingly this revolt was centered on a figure claiming to be the Messiah, Simon bar Kochba. It all ended with the calamity of the siege at the cliff top fortress at Masada, housing the last remnants of the revolt.

46. See especially Jacob Neusner's magisterial study, <u>The Rabbinic Traditions about the Pharisees before 70</u>, 3 vols., E. J. Brill, Leiden, 1971.

47. Orthodox Judaism: all halakah is binding on all Jews; Conservative Judaism: some halakah is adaptable by the community; Reform Judaism: all halakah is non-binding and each individual is free to decide what to observe, and Reconstruction Judaism: such halakah as the individual accepts is followed only to preserve Jewish civilization. See the point about "Judaisms" in note 38. Christian denominationalism and the fracturing of Christian orthodoxy in the late 20th and early 21st centuries points to the reality of "Christianities" also. I shall be returning to this point in this book's companion volume.

48. The Gospels "begin" the New Testament in print order alone. Most scholars are of the view that they were written after Paul's letters.

49. There is no evidence in Roman records of such a census. Luke's concern to say when, as distinct from where, Jesus was born is more clearly indicated by his placing it (as does Matthew) during the reign of Herod the Great. Herod is reported to have died between what we now refer to as 6 and 4 BCE. There never was a year "0" and the division of epochs into BCE and CE or BC and AD came only very much later, following the work of an English scholar, Bede. Bede worked around the year 800 CE and in calculating the date of Herod's death made an error. Thus the calendars that followed are out by four to six years. The changes of our years, decades, centuries, and millennia are the result of a thirteen-hundred-year-old mistake. To pour any divine significance into these changes of years, decades, centuries, and even millennia is superstition in the extreme.

50. Hebrew today can be pronounced in two very different ways. One, the Ashkenazi, follows the tradition of northern European Jewry, while the other, the Sephardic, follows the Jewish traditions of the Iberian Peninsula. In Ashkenazi pronunciation the Hebrew "th" and "t" sounds tend to become "s." Thus, we hear *shabbas* instead of *shabat* and *bris* instead of *brit* for the rite of circumcision.

51. While there are three types of gift, there is no specific number given to the *magoi*. Christian legend quickly identified them as three, however, based on more than the three types of gift. This event is celebrated in the church as the Epiphany of Christ. As we saw with Antiochus Epiphanes, epiphany means "manifestation" and this feast is thus the Feast of the Manifestation of Christ to the Nations, in fulfillment, of course, of the Abrahamic promise. The Bible after the flood refers to all peoples descending from the sons of Noah, of whom there were three, namely Shem, Ham, and Japheth. This is the foundation for the number three being assigned to these *magoi*. Many Christian artists take this imagery even further portraying the three as of three different races.

52. The Greek in this passage uses a word, *paidion*, which throughout Greek is used of what we would call a toddler. The *magoi* did not visit a newborn infant. This also explains Herod's desire to slaughter all the male children "two years of age and younger" (Matt. 2:16).

53. To be in a position to maintain the doctrine of the perpetual virginity of Mary, the Roman Catholic tradition asserts, against the plain meaning of the texts, that the persons referred to in these passages are Jesus' cousins or the like.

54. See Geza Vermes, The Complete Dead Sea Scrolls in English, Penguin, London, 1991, p. 174.

55. Needless to say, a thorough treatment of this subject would require an entire book. I hope to provide that soon in terms of a study of Mark's Gospel.

56. See Robert H. Schuller, The Be (Happy) Attitudes: 8 Positive Attitudes That Can Transform Your Life, Word, Irving, 1985.

57. Notice how thoroughly Jesus affirms that actions can lead to life. This is a doctrine of works ("by your fruits you shall know them") at odds with many simplistic interpretations heard in some Christian circles today.

58. In Aristotelian philosophy we find the term "entelechy." It means the dynamic of a thing to reach the goal (its *telos*) of its being. It is a fancy word for self-realization. The wholeness Jesus makes possible is similar to, but in one key aspect, different from this. The *telos* of the self is to become, not all you want to be, but all God wants you to be and knows you can become. If I may be permitted to coin a word, the encountering summons to wholeness made possible in Jesus is theontelechy.

59. This is the ultimate meaning of the Incarnation.

60. See Neil Gillman, The Death of Death: Resurrection and Immortality in Jewish Thought, Jewish Lights Publishing, Woodstock, Vermont, 2000.

61. Compare Hyam Maccoby, <u>The Mythmaker: Paul and the Invention of Christianity</u>, Barnes and Noble, New York, 1986, and Alan F. Segal, <u>Paul the Convert: The Apostolate and Apostasy of Saul the Pharisee</u>, Yale University Press, New Haven, 1990.

62. The works of the Seminar are contained in two volumes, <u>The Five Gospels: What Did Jesus Really Say?</u> Macmillan, New York, 1993, and <u>The Acts of Jesus: What Did Jesus Really Do?</u>, Harper, San Francisco, 1998. The Seminar's method of making decisions is somewhat quaint. It is based on the tradition of using red ink for the authentic words of Jesus. After studying and discussing a passage, the seminar members would cast a vote in the form of a colored bead: red for "certainly by Jesus," pink for "possibly by Jesus," gray for "probably not by Jesus," and black for "certainly not." In the two volumes, needless to say, black ink predominates. Red ink is scarce. (Given the pressure in the churches to use gender neutral language I find it humorous at the least that across both versions of the Lord's Prayer, the Seminar uses red for only one word: "Father.")

63. The length of the delay in writing the Gospels can be explained by a combination of factors: first, the early Christians seemed to expect the return of Jesus imminently; second, the apostles were living and only after some time did it dawn on the church that these living witnesses would soon perish with their memories; and third, the expense of production needed to be met by a church that had gained enough affluence.

64. The reality of the persecutions suffered by the early Christians, from the middle 60s until the adoption of Christianity as the religion of the Empire in the early fourth century is almost beyond belief and description. If you are unfamiliar with this period of persecution and the price that was paid by these generations of Christians I urge you to peruse any good church history of this period. It is both a disturbing and deeply moving story.

65. In the Gospels, the Synoptics in general and Mark in particular, Jesus is pictured as surrounded by ever increasing concentric circles of companions. The innermost circle is made up of Peter, James, and John, sometimes including Andrew. Beyond this inner circle is the "twelve," the apostles, and beyond them a group called "disciples." Further out still are some referred to as "followers," beyond which is "the crowd." Beyond the crowd lies "all peoples."

66. This is not unlike the Islamic notion of *barzakh*.

67. Jesus was not dead for three days and nights. He died sometime late on Friday afternoon. The Jewish Sabbath (Saturday) began at sundown on Friday, say around 6 PM. This accounts for the haste to get Jesus' body down and buried, before the Sabbath, which prohibited such work. The next event we read of is the arrival at the tomb of some women (their identity is a matter of confusion amongst the four Gospels) at dawn on Sunday. He is not there, of course, and resurrection faith flows. Thus, how long was Jesus dead and buried? From, let us say, 4 PM on Friday to sometime before 6 AM on Sunday. Hardly, "three days." By one way of reckoning, of course, it can be said he rose "on the third day."

0-595-33813-5

Printed in the United States
43025LVS00004B/187-189

9 780595 338139